10th E

D1460174

Air
Traffic Control

Graham Duke

MIDLAND
An imprint of
Ian Allan Publishing

Contents

ACKNOWLEDGEMENTS
I wish to record my appreciation for the
help and co-operation I have received from
individuals and organisations in the
preparation of this volume, in particular:
Richard Wright, National Air Traffic
Services; Rick Boden and Andrew Burke,
London Area Control Centre, Swanwick;
Finlay Smith and Valerie Allan, Shanwick
Operations, Prestwick; Shaun Grist,
Newport; and to Enid for her co-operation
and patience throughout.

*Previous page: **The Central Tower at
London Heathrow.** NATS*

First published 2009

ISBN 978 1 85780 318 1

Published by Midland Publishing

an imprint of Ian Allan Publishing Ltd, Hersham, Surrey
KT12 4RG.
Printed in England by Ian Allan Printing Ltd, Hersham,
Surrey KT12 4RG.

Code: 0908/B3

Visit the Ian Allan Publishing website at
www.ianallanpublishing.co.uk

1. Introduction – An Overview

Suddenly, in the summer of 2008, the steady increase in European air traffic began to slow as the crisis in the world financial markets started to bite. In August, for the first time, traffic levels fell. This followed a period of growth since the downturn after the events of September 2001, and was the result of several factors including a contraction of disposable income and a steep rise in fuel costs.

Almost every airline was affected, resulting in some routes being cut. However, in spite of this, forecasters predict that traffic levels will recover to 2007 levels (possibly by 2011) and are likely to continue to increase over the next 15 years, putting pressure on air navigation service providers throughout Europe to maintain and even improve safety levels and also cut delays.

Even so, annual traffic levels in UK airspace now stand at 2.5 million flights, compared with 1 million in 1985.

The European Organisation for the Safety of Air Navigation, EUROCONTROL, based in Brussels, is at the forefront of a package of measures which will incease capacity while at the same time reducing delays and improving safety.

The foundation for these ambitious improvements is the Single European Sky Air Traffic Management Research Programme (SESAR), which aims to treble capacity by 2020 through the development of systems that will accommodate traffic flying on tracks that operate in four dimensions.

The Definition phase of SESAR was finalised in 2008, and the Development phase will take until 2013 to complete. This will be followed by the Deployment phase, planned for completion in 2020.

By 2020, EUROCONTROL aims to increase capacity through the use of advanced technology while also improving safety by a factor of 10, reducing harmful emissions by 10 per cent and cutting air traffic management costs by as much as 50 per cent.

Eurocontrol Experimental Centre
Eurocontrol

Terminal 5, London Heathrow Author

EUROCONTROL is collaborating with other organisations around the world in order to achieve a global solution. In America, for example, under the Next Generation Air Transportation System (NextGen) programme, the Federal Aviation Administration aims to fundamentally overhaul US airspace and introduce advanced technology to meet future demand and improve safety.

However, these proposals require a major investment by all concerned if they are to become effective, and there is concern that the programme is in danger of stalling as the airlines and governments look for ways of cutting costs.

Managing the Airspace

National Air Traffic Services (NATS) is the organisation responsible for air traffic management in UK airspace. It was separated from the Civil Aviation Authority in 2001, under a controversial public/private partnership, when the Government sold off 51 per cent of the business, retaining a 49 per cent interest.

Today, the Airline Group holds a 42 per cent share, British Airports Authority a 4 per cent share, and an Employers Share Trust has the remaining 5 per cent.

In March 2003 the financial restructuring of NATS was completed, with an investment of £65 million each from the British Airports Authority and the Government. This had been necessary following the downturn in business after the terrorist attacks in New York in 2001.

Under the terms of its licence, NATS is required to be capable of meeting on a continuous basis any reasonable level of overall demand. The organisation is charged with permitting access to airspace on behalf of all users, whilst making the most efficient overall use of airspace.

Income for NATS is produced through internationally agreed charges for the flights that use UK airspace, based on the aircraft weight and the distance flown. For example, a B747 from the east coast of America to London will be charged around £550, while an Airbus A320 from Paris to London will pay around £100.

After a turbulent few years since privatisation, NATS finally moved into the black during the twelve-month period to 31 March 2004, with an £1.8 million profit, compared with a £29.1 million loss the previous year and a £79.9 million loss the year before that.

TRY SOMETHING DIFFERENT

Scanning?
Listening?
Try Transmitting?

Many think of becoming an amateur radio operator as something hard to achieve but this just isn't the case. Amateur radio in the UK has never been more accessible and you could easily be on the air talking to the world right now. All UK licences provide access to a wide range of radio bands including HF for worldwide communications, in fact through the spectrum from microwaves to LF.

Amateur radio is endlessly fascinating and getting "on the air" opens a whole new world to you, enabling you to make friends all over the world, build your own equipment, install your own amateur radio station and participate in the hobby in whatever way you want. You could try:

✔ Emergency Communications
✔ Amateur Radio Satellites
✔ International Space Station
✔ Data Communication
✔ Direction Finding
✔ Contests
✔ Awards
✔ And much, much, more!

All that is needed is a pass at Foundation level to access amateur radio and this can be achieved in as little as a weekend. The Foundation level even provides training in basic operating that gets you "on the air", so you know how to operate when you get a licence. All that is required beyond the practical elements provided in the training is that you pass a straightforward test of 25 multiple choice questions. There is nothing to be frightened of in the exam either, as we have had thousands pass in recent years, with some as young as 7 going on to be licensed radio amateurs.

There is nothing to stop you expanding your horizons so why not get into amateur radio?

For more information visit **www.rsgb.org/getlicence** or ring 01234 832 700 to be sent details of training and exams in your area.

This article was brought to you by the Radio Society of Great Britain
3 Abbey Court, Fraser Road, Priory Business Park, Bedford, MK44 3WH
Tel: 01234 832 700

At the end of the financial year 2007/8, NATS recorded its fifth year of profit.

At the same time, there has been a very considerable reduction in the flight delays which can be attributed to NATS. In 2007, 97.6 per cent of flights handled by NATS were not delayed, while the average delay per flight for the whole year was 24 seconds, compared with 2.5 minutes in 2002 and 11 minutes in 1993.

The improvement in safety levels is also significant. The number of Airproxes in UK airspace (incidents where the safety of aircraft may have been compromised) is only 20 per cent of the number reported in 1997, despite the increased traffic volume. In 2007, there were five Airproxes which were judged to be risk bearing and only one of these was attributed to NATS.

Controller Shortage

Another issue that needs to be urgently addressed is the huge worldwide shortage of controllers, due in part to several States deciding to reduce or even stop the recruitment of new controllers following the events of September 2001 and the subsequent downturn.

In Europe, there are estimated to be over 1,000 unfilled vacancies, while in the US, of the 14,000 controllers currently employed, around 11,000 will become eligible for retirement between 2008 and 2011.

Urgent action to encourage new applicants into the profession is recognised by EUROCONTROL and the FAA, as well as other air navigation service providers. However, becoming a controller today does not seem to attract as many new entrants as in the past.

Various reasons have been suggested for this, including the perceived stress levels associated with busy and complex airspace, unsocial hours, publicity over safety-related incidents and the threat of prosecution or sanctions if something goes wrong. The failure rate is also high, with at least 40 per cent of new entrants being dismissed before the end of their training.

Although the delay per flight in UK airspace has improved considerably, the same cannot be said for the whole of Europe. Between 1999 and 2009, the European airspace capacity increased by almost 50 per cent while traffic levels rose by just under a quarter, but the average en route delay for the summer of 2008 increased to 2 minutes, double the target set by EUROCONTROL.

This increased delay is mainly the result of a lack of ATM capacity due to insufficient numbers of available controllers, resulting in some sectors remaining closed or at best undermanned. Other factors include the the a postponement of improvement programmes

Air France A320-211 Shaun Grist

Eurocontrol Experimental Centre
Eurocontrol

at some ATC centres and the limitations of certain systems.

Overall for the first time in ten years, the available European airspace capacity in the summer of 2008 declined by 2 per cent. This is not forecast to improve until at least 2011, one of the primary reasons being the shortage of controllers.

Do You Read?

One area of concern, affecting pilots and controllers alike, is the increasing number of incidents where language has been proved to be a factor. Although English is the international standard for aviation communication, the inability to speak and understand messages, especially in non-standard situations, has caused numerous safety-related problems.

This has been recognised by the International Civil Aviation Organization (ICAO) and in 2003 its requirements for a minimum standard of language proficiency (applicable to all aviation languages, not just English) were adopted and published.

In Europe, EUROCONTROL has decreed that by May 2010 all controllers operating in Europe must demonstrate a satisfactory standard of the English language through a process entitled ELPAC – English Language Proficiency for Aeronautical Communication.

Under ELPAC, a series of tests have been developed which will focus on the use of language, not the ATC procedures. Controllers who are unable to pass these tests run the risk of having their licences suspended or even removed. The tests involve speaking to pilots and to other controllers, and listening to messages which may not always use standard phraseology, especially in unusual circumstances. A variety of sample tests are available via the internet for controllers to familiarise themselves with the test material.

Terminal 5, London Heathrow Author

Eurocontrol Institute of Air Navigation Services Eurocontrol

Moving Towards a Two-Centre Strategy

Since the London Area Control Centre at Swanwick in Hampshire opened for business on 27 January 2002, it has enjoyed a period of excellent performance, demonstrated by the fact that safety-related incidents and delays have been reduced to a record low. It is recognised as a world leader in air traffic management, even though there have been the occasional software problems which have resulted in short-term delays and frustration for many passengers and airlines.

In November 2007, the London Terminal Control function moved from West Drayton, near Heathrow, to a dedicated Operations Room at the London Area Control Centre, completing the final stage of development at Swanwick.

At Prestwick, Scotland, work on a new Scottish en route centre is virtually complete. It will be fully operational in 2010, incorporating the ATC function from Manchester Control Centre (which will close) – the culmination of the Two-Centre Strategy for UK airspace.

Making the Changes

Airspace management is a fluid, responsive and ever-changing environment. Apart from the long-term goals forecast for many years into the future, a continuous programme of improvement takes place affecting routes and airspace design.

Airways are frequently subject to modification, new routes are being introduced, new reporting points established and the re-design of segments of airspace is an ongoing exercise. The largest consultation ever involved the airspace in an area to the northeast of London (so called Terminal Control North) during which NATS invited comments from interested parties and a population of around 12 million in the affected areas. During the 17-week consultation, NATS distributed around 1,500 documents, 3,000 DVDs and half a million leaflets.

The results were taken into account before NATS decided to revise its proposals and conduct a further consultation which will include the use of Precision Area Navigation (P-RNAV) routes.

Other consultation exercises involved the airspace in the Irish Sea area and in the

The London Area Control Centre, Swanwick

Bournemouth/Isle of Wight region in southern England.

NATS is very much involved with moving forward with the Single European Sky, collaborating with its European partners in the development of advanced procedures and systems. The UK and Irish authorities were the first to combine parts of their airspace into one integrated unit, known as a Functional Airspace Block (FAB), a process intended to improve the performance of air traffic, create shorter and more efficient routes, reduce the environmental impact and improve safety.

In Europe, a major FAB is planned for the central area of the continent under an agreement between the air navigation service providers of Belgium, France, Germany, Luxembourg, the Netherlands and Switzerland, to be known as Functional Airspace Block Europe Central (FABEC).

This creation of a common airspace management system in the core area of Europe will handle over five million flights a year, amounting to 55 per cent of all European traffic.

Terminal Control Room, Swanwick NATS

Conclusion

This has been an overview of the UK/European air traffic management system, which will be explored in more detail throughout the remainder of the book.

It is written primarily for non-professionals and attempts to describe the systems and procedures in an informal way.

Much of the detail has been made available through the patience and generous assistance of many professionals in the world of aviation and air traffic control. Without exception, everyone has been particularly helpful and encouraging, and I am pleased to record my gratitude to them.

Air traffic management is an evolving process, with ambitious plans for the future needed to meet the challenges of an increasing demand from the travelling public. Moves towards the implementation of new technology are already well under way and these will have significant effects on capacity, safety and environmental improvements.

Airband Listening

For anyone interested in the hobby of airband listening and tracking, a companion book on the subject is available, also published by Midland. Entitled *Airband Radio Guide*, now in its seventh edition, it gives detailed information on how to get the best results from the available equipment.

The London Area Control Centre, Swanwick, Hampshire Author

Singapore Airlines A380 preparing to line up on 09R at London Heathrow Author

2. Airspace Essentials

The safe conduct of flight is the first priority of any air traffic service. At the same time, many pilots do not want to have to follow strict and inflexible rules while in the air. These opposing requirements are met by dividing airspace into two basic types.

Firstly, some airspace is designed to allow the safe and expeditious flights of passenger-carrying aircraft, linking airports and continents through a system of airways and high-level routes, under the continuous surveillance and protection of an air traffic control service.

Secondly, the remaining airspace is free for any pilot to use as he or she wishes (subject to certain basic rules of the air), without hindrance or interference from controllers.

This basic and simple principle is applied across UK airspace, although in order to ensure that it meets everyone's needs a number of intermediate stages are necessary.

Qantas B747 Author

Division of Airspace

Airspace is divided into a number of categories, with a variety of definitions, many of them completely invisible to pilots. Some of the categories are linked to the European harmonisation process designed to streamline air traffic management and efficiency.

Firstly, UK airspace consists of two regions:
- England and Wales – London Flight Information Region (FIR)
- Scotland and Northern Ireland – Scottish Flight Information Region (FIR)

These regions are then subdivided into upper and lower airspace, with a further subdivision into smaller areas, or sectors.

Lower airspace consists of a number of regulated and unregulated categories, where the degree of control exercised by air traffic controllers varies considerably. Outside regulated (or controlled) airspace, the service offered to pilots is designed to give them maximum autonomy and flexibility.

Each of these categories is explained in more detail in this chapter.

Flight Information Regions

As mentioned above, the airspace of England and Wales, and the surrounding sea areas, is known as the London FIR. The airspace of Scotland and Northern Ireland, and the surrounding sea areas, is known as the Scottish FIR.

Within each region, the term FIR relates to the airspace below flight level 245 (FL245, approximately 24,500ft).

Airspace at and above FL245 is known as the Upper Flight Information Region (UIR). However, it is common practice to refer to all airspace as the FIR.

The FIR/UIR titles 'London' and 'Scottish' are also used as the radio callsigns, although some parts of the airspace are delegated to other agencies – for example, traffic in the airspace in the Manchester area up to FL285 is the responsibility of Manchester Area Control Centre, using the callsign Manchester.

A separate FIR/UIR covers the Republic of Ireland, under the jurisdiction of the Irish Aviation Authority, using the callsign Shannon, although a new era of co-operation and collaboration between London and Shannon came into being in 2008 with the introduction of the first European Functional Airspace Block (FAB).

In addition, as part of the European programme of harmonisation, in line with other EUROCONTROL member states, FL195 was implemented in UK airspace in 2006. Although the division between upper and lower airspace still remains at FL245, this change means that all flights operating above FL195 are subject to air traffic surveillance and control.

The UK Airspace System

All airspace in the UK is divided into two main classifications: controlled and uncontrolled (often described as regulated and unregulated airspace).

The term 'controlled airspace' is applied to those parts of the system which are subject to certain rules and regulations. These rules are prescribed by National Air Traffic Services Limited, the Civil Aviation Authority and the international governing

Aircraft of Czech Airlines Czech Airlines

body, the International Civil Aviation Organization.

Pilots, and the aircraft they fly, must conform to a number of requirements regarding pilot qualifications, carriage of equipment, operating procedures, and so on before they can operate in certain controlled airspace.

There are a number of categories of controlled airspace, which are described in detail later. The rules vary considerably in each type, including some where the flight may not be under positive control; this is why controlled airspace is sometimes described more realistically as regulated airspace.

Outside the controlled parts of the system the airspace is described as uncontrolled or free airspace. Very few Air Traffic Control rules apply in these cases. Outside controlled airspace pilots may fly where they wish, without mandatory control, provided they comply with a series of common-sense rules, designed to afford an appropriate level of protection without being unduly restrictive.

Controlled, or regulated, airspace is designed to protect aircraft in flight, both in the en route phase and when departing or approaching airports. However, at some of the smaller airports, which are increasingly being used by some low-cost carriers, the volume of traffic and the types of flight may not justify the creation of controlled airspace.

However, this means that passenger-carrying jets have to pass through

Visual Control Room, Bristol Author

uncontrolled airspace (where there could be other unknown aircraft) to reach their destination.

This issue is, of course, being monitored by the responsible authorities. When traffic reaches a level where there is an increasing risk, the question of creating controlled airspace is considered.

One example of this concerned the airspace surrounding the airports at Cardiff and Bristol, where arrivals and departures had to cross through uncontrolled airspace without the benefit of the safety net offered by controllers. The increasing volume of commercial traffic and the associated risks meant that action was needed.

Consequently, in August 2006 a new area of controlled airspace was implemented, covering both airports with links to the adjacent airways system. At the same time, the control of the airspace in the region, up to FL165, was delegated to Cardiff ATC. This area is the largest in the UK where Swanwick has delegated the control function to airport controllers. Similar developments were also implemented at Newcastle.

Sectorisation

UK airspace is subdivided into a number of geographical regions – some very large, others quite small – known as sectors. Generally, the size of a sector is dictated by the anticipated traffic levels that can be safely managed by a team of controllers. Within the boundaries of each of these sectors, traffic in controlled airspace is under the jurisdiction of a team of controllers operating from one of the appropriate control centres. Each sector normally has an allocation of one main civil radio frequency and one or two reserve frequencies. As a flight proceeds through the airspace, responsibility passes from one sector team to the next, with controllers instructing pilots to switch to the next sector radio frequency.

Information on each flight is automatically generated and presented to the controllers some 15 minutes before it enters the sector. This information is in the form of Flight Progress Strips – thin pieces of card mounted on plastic holders – or alternatively as an electronic version displayed on a screen. As instructions are issued to pilots, the details are marked on the strips either by pen or electronically.

Airspace Classifications

There are seven internationally agreed categories of airspace, identified by the letters A, B, C, D, E, F and G. There is no requirement for every State to adopt all seven types. This is dependent on the individual circumstances in its region.

The first six categories (Classes A, B, C, D, E and F) are controlled (or regulated) airspace, where air traffic controllers have certain duties and responsibilities, and where the airspace is subject to a number of rules.

Class G airspace is uncontrolled (or free) airspace, where there are no ATC rules, although there are numerous 'Rules of the Air'. Generally, pilots may operate in Class G airspace without expecting any restrictions or limitations on their flight, but they are always responsible for collision avoidance and terrain clearance.

Controllers never refer to the airspace classification system. Instead, their messages will only mention controlled or uncontrolled airspace.

Around aerodromes, the airspace contained within an area of 2.5 nautical miles (nm) radius and extending from the surface up to a height of 2,000ft (known as an Aerodrome Traffic Zone) is automatically in the same class as the surrounding area.

Airways

The airways system consists of corridors of protected airspace which enable commercial and military transport aircraft to route across the country with the benefit of a continuous control service, aided by radar or some other surveillance system, in which ground-based controllers assume responsibility for the safe separation of the various flights within their sector. The routes are defined by radio navigation beacons dotted around the country. Controllers issue instructions by radiotelephone to the pilots of aircraft within the airways and those instructions must be followed.

Airways are at least ten nautical miles in width, with an upper level of FL245. However, the base levels of airways can vary considerably, from FL50 (5,000ft) to FL150 (15,000ft) or more. Each airway is designed to accommodate the needs of the traffic that will use it, which is why the base levels are so varied. (Note that the airspace between FL195 and FL245 is Class C – see below.)

Outside the airway, the airspace is uncontrolled and aircraft are not normally permitted to stray beyond the limits of the airway.

Air Canada B777 Author

Classes of Airspace

CLASS A

This provides the highest level of protection, where controllers are responsible for ensuring that safe separation between all aircraft is maintained at all times.

This means that:

- all flights must be flown under Instrument Flight Rules
- flight plans are mandatory
- Air Traffic Control instructions must be followed
- radios must be monitored at all times
- transponders must be operating in height readout mode (known as Mode C*)
- aircraft with 19 or more seats must be operating TCAS* equipment.

(* these terms are described later)

In certain circumstances, flights which are being flown visually may be permitted to enter Class A airspace. This is usually under 'Special VFR' conditions.

Class A airspace applies to the following (with an upper limit of FL195):

- all airways (there are a few exceptions)
- the Channel Islands Control Area
- Clacton Control Area
- Daventry Control Area
- London Terminal Manoeuvring Area
- London Control Zone
- Manchester Terminal Manoeuvring Area
- North Sea Control Area
- Shanwick Oceanic Control Area
- Worthing Control Area.

CLASS B

No UK airspace is designated as Class B.

CLASS C

This applies to all UK airspace above FL195, affording a high level of protection, where controllers are responsible for ensuring the safe separation between all aircraft.

There are no airways in upper airspace (i.e. above FL245), only straight-line routes between navigation points, which are often not supported by radio facilities on the ground. Controllers frequently authorise aircraft to fly on tracks which do not follow these routes while at the same time remaining in fully controlled airspace at all times.

In March 2006, Class C airspace was implemented above FL245 as a replacement for Class B airspace.

On 15 March 2007, to bring the UK into line with the rest of Europe, the upper limit for Class C airspace was lowered to FL195. This was necessary to comply with a European ruling that had a deadline of 1 July 2007.

However, the division between upper and lower airspace in the UK remains at FL245. This means that an airway is designated Class A up to FL195, and Class C between FL195 and FL245.

The CAA accepts that certain VFR flights still need to operate between FL195 and FL245, and to accommodate these flights Temporary Reserved Areas were introduced in eight locations across the UK.

In addition, in airspace which is authorised for reduced vertical separation (as in the UK) international rules do not permit VFR flights.

CLASS D

This covers most airport control area and control zones, with the exception of those in the London and Manchester TMAs, which are Class A.

Class D airspace is designed to accommodate a mix of commercial transport flights and small general aviation aircraft which operate from many aerodromes. Therefore, both IFR and VFR flights are allowed, although VFR flights may be refused permission to enter the airspace if the controllers are too busy.

In Class D airspace, ATC will provide separation between all IFR flights. IFR flights will also be given traffic information about VFR flights, but not separation.

VFR flights will be given information about IFR flights and other VFR flights, but they will not be separated from other traffic.

Separation between IFR and VFR flights, and between VFR flights, is the responsibility of the pilots, under the 'see and avoid principle'. In other words, the pilot of a VFR

flight must keep a good lookout at all times as he is ultimately responsible for collision avoidance and terrain clearance.

The rules in Class D airspace are:
- flight plans are required (but may be given over the radio)
- ATC clearance is required
- Radio monitoring is required
- ATC instructions are mandatory.

CLASS E
Class E airspace covers the Belfast TMA, Glasgow Control Area, Durham Tees Valley Control Zone and parts of the Scottish TMA below 6000ft.

The rules are similar to those in Class D, except that traffic information is given only to VFR pilots who request it.

IFR flights will be separated from each other, and traffic information will be given to IFR pilots concerning VFR flights which are known to the controller.

VFR pilots do not have to obtain a clearance from ATC, or contact them by radio, although they are encouraged to do so.

CLASS F
This covers Advisory Routes in UK airspace.

Controllers will provide advice on separation between those IFR flights which are known to the controller.

Transavia B737 – 7K2
Shaun Grist

Advisory Routes are those used by civil flights but which do not carry the volume of traffic sufficient to justify the status of an airway. Class F airspace covers all Advisory Routes in the UK.

On these routes the controller will provide a limited service (not full control) to those aircraft participating in the service to ensure that the rules of separation are applied. The service is available to flights below FL195, but may be reduced at low levels due to the inadequate cover of the radar. In such cases it may be possible for pilots to receive a service from a military airfield in the vicinity.

Advisory Routes are designated on low-level charts with a letter 'D' – for example, W958D is Advisory Route 'Whiskey Nine Five Eight Delta'.

There are currently around 15 Advisory Routes in UK airspace.

The rules (applicable to participating flights) are:
- flight plans are required (but may be given over the radio)
- ATC clearance is required
- radio communication is required
- ATC instructions are mandatory.

CLASS G

Class G applies to all airspace not included in any of the other classes.

There are no ATC rules concerning flight plans, radios or clearances. However, pilots who are in contact with ATC are expected to follow their instructions. If this is not possible the pilot must inform the controller.

A pilot must obtain permission before entering an Aerodrome Traffic Zone, or other area of controlled airspace, either by radio or some other means.

Pilots must also comply with the various rules concerning the use of transponders (above FL100) and the quadrantal flight levels, which are explained later.

In Class G airspace, large areas of the UK are covered by the Lower Airspace Radar Service (LARS) which is provided by certain civil and military airfields. Although this service is not mandatory, most pilots contact LARS when on cross-country flights.

The Flight Information Service (FIS) is a non-radar service operated from the London and Scottish centres, providing basic information on flights known to the controller. An additional Flight Information Service for the London area is operated from Farnborough.

Pilots flying in Class G Airspace (often referred to as free airspace) may request assistance from an Air Traffic Service Unit if they so desire. There are four available types of service, which will be covered later.

UK Flight Information Services

This is the official title of a new suite of services, known commonly as Air Traffic Services Outside Controlled Airspace (ATSOCAS) which came into effect on 12 March 2009. Full details are set out in Civil Aviation Publication CAP 774.

Background

Following a number of investigations by the Air Accidents Investigation Board, it became clear that many general aviation pilots and air traffic controllers were uncertain about the services they could expect or deliver when operating outside controlled airspace. In addition, questions and comments made at CAA Safety Evening meetings confirmed this fact, and even among air traffic service providers themselves there was evidence that there were many misunderstandings and contradictions.

Part of the problem originated from the fact that the rules governing the services provided by civil controllers and their military counterparts were based on separate sets of regulations. Furthermore, some of the basic rules had been modified to meet local circumstances. The control techniques and phraseology used by different ATS units also varied, adding to the confusion and misunderstandings.

It was apparent that there was a need for a review and a complete overhaul of the types of service available for flights outside controlled airspace, and most importantly, for one single set of rules which could be applied to any airspace user – transport flights, general aviation and the military. It was also accepted that the services should primarily meet the needs of the airspace user.

The new services were developed by the Airspace and Safety Initiative, consisting of representatives of the Civil Aviation Authority, National Air Traffic Services, Airports Operating Authority, general aviation and the Ministry of Defence. Consultation with interested parties commenced in late 2007, which included an interactive web-based training pack, and over 400 responses were received.

The rules apply to flights in Class F and Class G airspace, and replace the previous services – Flight Information, Radar Information, Radar Advisory and Class F Advisory Services.

There are four types of service, offering various degrees of information, advice or deconfliction in order to help the pilot avoid collisions:
- Basic Service
- Traffic Service
- Deconfliction Service
- Procedural Service.

The principles of the services are as follows:
- Where aircraft are operating outside controlled airspace (i.e. in Class F and Class G airspace) it is not mandatory for an air traffic service to be provided; therefore pilots are solely responsible for collision avoidance and terrain clearance *at all times*.
- Controllers and Flight Information Service Officers (FISOs) should try to give the service requested by the pilot but may not always be able to do so.
- FISOs may only provide the Basic Service, and only when an aircraft is outside an aerodrome.
- Controllers and pilots can agree between them that an aircraft will operate at a certain level, level band, heading, route or operating area.

Sometimes controllers will be unable to pass traffic information due to workload, the traffic environment or equipment limitations, and in such cases the pilot should be informed. For example, transponding aircraft may not be seen by a controller using primary radar.

Basic Service

A Basic Service can be requested under any conditions, although it is not considered

Egypt Air B777 – 266ER
Shaun Grist

appropriate for flights in IMC if there are other services available.

ATCOs or FISOs may pass relevant information to assist the pilot to achieve safe and efficient flight – for example, weather, serviceability of facilities, aerodrome information and general activity in the area, such as gliding.

Pilots should not expect traffic information automatically, but a warning may be given if there appears to be a definite risk. However, the pilot must not presume that the flight is being monitored.

ATCOs may use radar, but it is not a condition that they do. Pilots may change headings, levels or routes without informing ATC unless they have formed an agreement.

The pilot is solely responsible for avoiding other traffic and terrain *at all times*.

Traffic Service

A Traffic Service is the Basic Service plus the following:

ATCOs give pilots traffic information on conflicting aircraft based on the use of surveillance (for example, radar), but no advice on remaining clear of other traffic is

given, and the pilot remains responsible for collision avoidance and terrain clearance at all times.

Note that a Traffic Service cannot be provided by FISOs.

Traffic information will be given where the controller believes the traffic will pass within three nm and 3,000ft of the subject aircraft, but no advice on avoidance will be given. Also, as the information may be late, or not given at all, the pilot must always keep a good lookout. Ideally, the traffic information should be given before the aircraft are within five nm of each other, but again this cannot be guaranteed.

The service may be provided under any flight rules or conditions, although it may not be suitable for flights in IMC. An aircraft receiving a Traffic Service must be identified by ATC through the use of transponder codes or turns. Headings and/or levels may be given for positioning an aircraft.

Deconfliction Service

A Deconfliction Service is the Basic Service plus the following:

Pilots are given traffic information and deconfliction advice, but avoiding other aircraft is still the pilot's responsibility. (Deconfliction means ensuring, as far as

Air India (Fly Globespan)
B767 –319ER Shaun Grist

reasonably possible, that an aircraft remains clear of other aircraft by the minimum prescribed distances).

The service may only be provided by air traffic controllers using a surveillance system and is available under any flight conditions or meteorological conditions.

A Deconfliction Service cannot be provided by FISOs.

The aircraft must be identified by the controller by the use of transponder codes or turns. Controllers will expect the pilot to accept headings or levels that may take the aircraft into cloud.

The deconfliction minima may not always be achieved due to workload or other reasons – for example, an unexpected change of direction or level by other aircraft.

Pilots can choose not to accept deconfliction advice, but should tell the controller if this is the case. Similarly, the controller should be informed before the pilot changes the aircraft's level or heading, unless safety is at risk.

Deconfliction advice or avoiding action may also include a reminder about terrain clearance.

Procedural Service

A Procedural Service is the Basic Service plus the following:

Instructions are issued by controllers in order to achieve minimum separation from other aircraft which are also receiving a procedural service from the same controller.

A Procedural Service cannot be provided by FISOs, and is a non-surveillance service – that is, without the use of radar.

The avoidance of other aircraft is still the pilot's responsibility.

The controller will provide vertical, lateral, longitudinal and time instructions so as to achieve safe separation from other aircraft under his control. However, other aircraft, not under control, may appear without warning, so pilots must keep a good look out at all times.

Where aircraft are operating in the vicinity of aerodromes, pilots are strongly advised to contact the relevant air traffic unit.

A Procedural Service may be requested under any flight rules or meteorological conditions and pilots will be expected to accept headings or levels which may take the aircraft into cloud. Therefore, pilots who do not wish to be given deconfliction advice should not ask for a procedural service.

Also, pilots in receipt of a Procedural Service will be expected to comply with time restraints, so it may not be an appropriate service for pilots who are using only visual references.

The minimum distances between aircraft under a Procedural Service are 1,000ft vertically or 500ft if operating in accordance with the Quadrantal Rule.

As the service is provided without the benefit of radar the controller has to depend on the accuracy of the position reports given by the pilots.

Aircraft do not need to be identified by the controller providing a Procedural Service, but a squawk code may be allocated for the benefit of other ATC units using radar. However, allocating a squawk code does not imply that a surveillance service is being provided.

The controller will give traffic information to pilots in receipt of the Basic Service, and also to pilots of other flights he may be aware of, but pilots are responsible for collision avoidance at all times.

Pilots should also remember that other traffic receiving the service may be co-ordinated; therefore they should not change level or heading without informing the controller.

Flight conditions and flight rules

Flight conditions relate to the prevailing weather, defining minimum flight visibility and distances from cloud.

There are two types of flight conditions:
- Visual Meteorological Conditions (VMC) (sometimes abbreviated to 'Victor Mike')
- Instrument Meteorological Conditions (IMC) (sometimes abbreviated to 'India Mike')

For flights operating in Visual Meteorological Conditions the regulations specify that the aircraft must maintain prescribed minimum distances from cloud, both horizontally and vertically, and different flight visibilities.

In most cases, for flights at or above FL100, the visibility must be at least 8km. Below FL100 the minimum visibility is usually 5km. Distances from cloud are typically 1,500m horizontally and 1,000ft vertically (note the use of metres and feet).

These requirements may vary according to:
- the class of airspace
- the speed of the aircraft
- the level of the aircraft
- the type of aircraft
- whether passengers are being carried.

In addition, in the case of low-level flights (at or below 3,000ft) the pilot must always be in sight of the surface.

If these conditions cannot be met, then Instrument Meteorological Conditions (IMC) apply.

A pilot who intends to fly in controlled airspace in IMC must have an instrument rating. In addition, if the controlled airspace is Class A or C, the pilot must operate the aircraft under Instrument Flight Rules regardless of the weather conditions.

There are also two types of flight rules. These define the rules which apply to pilots according to the conditions of their licences.

- Visual Flight Rules (VFR) apply where the conditions set out above can be complied with.
- Instrument Flight Rules (IFR) apply where those conditions cannot be met, or where the flight is conducted in Class A or Class C airspace.

Pilots who are not qualified to fly on instruments, or who intend flying an aircraft which is not certified for instrument flight, may only do so if they can remain at all times within the appropriate minimum weather conditions specified for VFR flight.

It is the pilot's responsibility to comply with the privileges of his licence, including pre-planning the flight based on current weather forecasts and in accordance with the Rules of the Air. Air traffic controllers will not give an opinion on the suitability of the flight conditions.

In addition, if a VFR flight is to take place in Class D or Class E airspace, the pilot must:
- file a flight plan
- keep a listening watch on the radio
- comply with ATC instructions.

Instrument Flight Rules are as follows:
- An aircraft must be flown at least 1,000ft above the highest obstacle within five nm of the estimated position of the aircraft, except that if the aircraft is at 3,000ft or below, it must be clear of cloud and in sight of the surface.
- In controlled airspace, the aircraft must be flown at the appropriate semicircular level unless authorised by ATC.
- Outside controlled airspace, the aircraft must be flown at a level which is in accordance with the Quadrantal Rule, unless the flight is at 3,000ft or below.
- Pilots must be trained and qualified to conduct the flight without any visual references and to use ground-based navigation aids and other facilities.

Other rules will also apply, depending on the type of airspace, regarding flight plans, keeping a listening watch and complying with ATC instructions.

Night flights
VFR flights are not permitted at night; therefore a pilot who wishes to fly at night in VMC in uncontrolled airspace must follow the Instrument Flight Rules. The rules also

Tunisair A320 – 211 Shaun Grist

require that a pilot flying at night must have a 'night rating' or an instrument rating.

Special VFR (SVFR)
In certain situations, the rules requiring a flight in a control zone to be conducted in accordance with Instrument Flight Rules may be relaxed, provided the traffic conditions and the controller's workload will allow this to be done safely. This is known as Special VFR.

An aircraft under Special VFR may be flown at night. The pilot must also at all times remain clear of cloud and in sight of the surface, and comply with ATC instructions.

ATC will not normally issue a Special VFR clearance to an aircraft intending to depart from an aerodrome within a control zone if the visibility is 1,800m or less, and/or the cloud ceiling is less than 600ft.

ATC will provide standard separation between SVFR flights and other IFR flights.

Specific requirements for individual control zones are published in the UK Aeronautical Publication, and other rules of the air still apply.

Within the London Control Area, special lanes exist in which VFR flights are handled under Special VFR conditions.

Military Flights
Military Aerodrome Traffic Zones (MATZ)
These protect the immediate vicinity of military airfields, extending from ground level to specified upper limits. The dimensions are generally five nm from the mid-point of the longest runway, extending from the surface up to 3,000ft, with one or possibly two stubs located on the runway centreline(s) measuring two nm either side of the centreline, five nm in length and extending from 1,000ft to 3,000ft.

Aircraft wishing to transit a MATZ should request such a clearance when at 15 nm or five minutes' flying time from the edge of the MATZ.

Restricted Areas
For operational reasons, especially military training, certain parts of UK airspace are not generally available to traffic operating outside controlled airspace. Some airspace is permanently out of bounds, while other parts are prohibited only at certain published times. These areas include Air-to-Air Refuelling Areas, Military Training Areas, Prohibited Areas, Restricted Areas, Danger Areas, Areas of Intense Aerial Activity, Aerial Tactics Areas, and Free Fall Parachute Drop Zones.

In some cases, flights may be given clearance to transit the area.

A number of Temporary Reserved Areas exist between FL195 and FL245 (which is Class C airspace) to permit its use by VFR traffic and military fast jets.

Military Flying
Military control units are based at the London and Scottish area control centres, as well as at military airfields. They are primarily responsible for military activity of all types, but they can, subject to workload, provide a service to civilian traffic operating in uncontrolled areas.

Royal Air Force personnel are also responsible for the Emergency Distress and Diversion cells.

Military transport flights often use the normal airways system where they will be under the control of the civil Air Traffic Control units with the normal requirements thus imposed, but military controllers at Air Traffic Control centres or military airfields handle the remaining aircraft.

Military pilots are not as restricted as their civilian colleagues since they must obviously be able to operate in a responsive and flexible environment as part of their operational needs.

Long-range routes do exist for use by the military, known as Tacan (Tactical Area Navigation) routes; they are indicated on Royal Air Force charts.

Military Traffic Categories
Military air traffic falls into one of two categories: General Air Traffic (GAT) and Operational Air Traffic (OAT).

The definition for GAT is that flights are conducted in accordance with the regulations and procedures for flight laid down by the civilian aviation authorities and operating under the same procedures as civilian air traffic.

Operational Air Traffic refers to flights which are under the control of a military Air Traffic Control authority.

It is possible for GAT traffic to become OAT traffic (or vice versa) as the flight transfers from one type of airspace to the other.

Royal Flights

Whenever a civil or military aircraft carries a member of the Royal Family in the UK, an area of protected airspace is created which is intended to ensure the safety of the Royal Flight throughout its journey.

The relevant members of the Royal Family are:
● Her Majesty The Queen
● His Royal Highness The Prince Philip, Duke of Edinburgh
● His Royal Highness The Prince of Wales
● Her Royal Highness The Duchess of Cornwall
● His Royal Highness The Prince William
● His Royal Highness The Duke of York
● His Royal Highness The Earl of Wessex
● Her Royal Highness The Countess of Wessex
● Her Royal Highness The Princess Royal.

However, it is also possible for other members of the Royal Family and for other sovereigns and heads of state to be included. Usually the Royal Flight will be routed along the normal UK airways system and through established control zones, but where this is not possible the flight will be afforded protection by the establishment of a Temporary Class A Controlled Airway, or CAS-T.

When it is necessary to depart from controlled airspace, a Temporary Airway, 10 nm wide, will be established for the flight. Similarly areas around airfields used by a Royal Flight will also be declared as Temporary Control Zones or Temporary Control Areas, both being Class A.

Where other traffic may be operating at an airfield where a Royal Flight is expected,

Military Control Operations Room, Swanwick NATS

Special VFR conditions will be applied to ensure the required separation.

The times allowed for CAS-T are from 15 minutes before the arrival or 30 minutes after the departure of the Royal Flight. The usual radio frequencies are used for a Royal Flight, but special ATC procedures apply to ensure separation from other flights.

CAS-T will not be applied where the Royal Flight is by helicopter. Instead, a Royal Low-Level Corridor will be established, with checkpoints at approximately 20 nm intervals. A 10-mile zone either side of the helicopter's track is applied to military aircraft, and they must at all times be laterally separated by 5 nautical miles from the Royal Flight, although this may be reduced to 3 nautical miles in certain circumstances.

Daily information on Temporary Controlled Airspace and other flying restrictions is available from the Aeronautical Information Service on telephone number 0500 354802.

Special arrangements exist for ensuring the safety of Royal and Selected helicopter flights, and for this purpose the major part of the UK landmass is subdivided into Safeguard Areas each of which has an associated Safeguard Unit. The units are responsible for the provision of an air traffic service to the flight in transit through the area by making use of all available facilities. The callsigns of Royal Flights identify those which are actually carrying Her Majesty the Queen or other members of the Royal Household.

The callsigns used by Royal Flights are as follows:

No 32 (The Royal) Squadron: *Kittyhawk* followed by a number and the letter 'R' if a member of the Royal Family is on board. (Positioning flights just use *Kitty*.)

The Queen's Helicopter Flight: *Rainbow* followed by a number and the letter 'R' if a member of the Royal Family is on board.

Civilian Chartered Aircraft: *Sparrowhawk* followed by a number and the letter 'R' if a member of the Royal Family is on board.

Civilian Chartered Rotary Wing Aircraft: *Sparrowhawk* followed by a number and the letter 'S' (only where the passengers have CAA priority and no member of the Royal Family is on board.)

Helicopters flown by HRH The Duke of York: *Leopard*.

Emergencies

Any pilot in difficulty or in urgent need of help whilst in flight may contact the Distress and Diversion Unit (D & D) at the London or Scottish Air Traffic Control centres on the International Aeronautical Emergency Frequencies (121.5 MHz VHF and 243.0 MHz UHF). These services are operated by military personnel on a continuous basis. The callsigns are London Centre or Scottish Centre as appropriate, although pilots needing assistance may not actually use them. When a pilot contacts the D & D cell at either centre, the position of the aircraft may be determined by direction-finding equipment located at various stations in the UK.

However, where an aircraft is already under the control of an air traffic unit, or is in communication with a controller (at an airfield, for example) the pilot will inform the controller of the nature of the emergency, using the normal VHF frequency. The controller should inform the D & D unit of the situation, but it may be appropriate for the subject aircraft to remain with the original controller for assistance.

For example, if a passenger aircraft routeing along an airway declares an emergency due to low fuel, the area controller handling traffic on the airway is probably in the best position to direct the aircraft to an airport for landing. In practice, the aircraft in distress may be given a dedicated airways frequency so that more undivided attention can be provided.

There are two classes of emergency message: Distress and Urgency.

Distress

A condition of being threatened by serious and/or imminent danger and requiring immediate assistance. The phrase used by the pilot to declare the emergency is 'May Day, May Day, May Day'. The callsign of the ATC is not usually given at this point.

Urgency

A condition concerning the safety of an aircraft or another vehicle, or of some person on board or within sight, but which does not require immediate assistance. The phrase used in this case is 'Pan-Pan, Pan-Pan, Pan-Pan'. (Note, however, that military pilots only say 'Pan-Pan'.) Again, the ATC callsign is not usually spoken.

Pilots may select the following transponder codes to indicate the emergency, or they may be requested to do so by the controller:
- Aircraft emergency – squawk 7700
- Radio failure – squawk 7600
- Hijack or other act of violence – squawk 7500.

However, if an aircraft in an emergency is already transponding on an operational code and is in communication with a controller, the pilot will not normally select any of the above codes unless he decides, or is advised, to do so.

Distress Messages

Depending on the circumstances, the distress traffic may be requested to change frequency by the controller to 121.5 MHz (VHF) or 243 MHz (UHF).

When a distress transmission is received on a frequency other than 121.5 MHz all other transmissions become secondary. The distress transmission is top priority and all other stations on that particular frequency must be silent.

When either of these frequencies is used, the precise position of the aircraft in trouble is automatically established by means of an auto-triangulation system. Direction-finding equipment based at Birmingham, Cardiff, Gatwick, Heathrow, Manchester, Stansted and nine military airfields, as well as units in Scotland, provides immediate information to the control centre where the details are instantly displayed on a high-definition VDU which has a database of full colour Ordnance Survey maps with airfields, navigation aids, radio beacons and so on included. Aircraft are identified by three radio direction fixes and one of the important advantages is that the aircraft does not have to carry a transponder.

The auto-triangulation system is operational in most of the UK, although its

Ryanair B737 – 8ASW Shaun Grist

effectiveness is reduced if the aircraft is below 5,000ft in the London FIR and 8,500ft in the Scottish FIR due to the proximity of high ground.

Where possible the following details should be included in the initial transmission, although where the aircraft is already under the control of an ATC unit some of the detail may be omitted:

- station being called
- callsign
- aircraft type
- nature of emergency
- intention of the person in command of the flight
- present position, flight level and heading qualifications of the pilot, i.e. student, IFR et cetera
- number of persons on board.

Pilots are at liberty to call the Distress and Diversion Unit at either London or Scottish control to practise an emergency situation provided actual emergencies are not affected. Additionally, pilots who are unsure of their position are encouraged to call D & D for assistance. In these circumstances the phrase used will be '*Practice Pan*' spoken three times.

Airproxes

In 1994 the UK Civil Aviation Authority adopted the ICAO term 'Airprox' to describe an incident that could have safety implications. The definition of Airprox is *'A situation in which, in the opinion of a pilot or a controller, the distance between aircraft as well as their relative positions and speed have been such that the safety of the aircraft involved was, or may have been, compromised.'*

There are four agreed categories:
A. Risk of collision – an actual risk of collision existed.
B. Safety not assured – the safety of the aircraft was compromised.
C. No risk of collision – no risk of collision existed.
D. Risk not determined – insufficient information was available to determine the risk involved, or inconclusive or conflicting evidence precluded such determination.

Inevitably, incidents occur which may compromise the safety of air travel, usually caused by errors or unforeseen events somewhere in the system. A tremendous amount of care and evaluation is exercised in designing, developing and implementing systems and procedures which limit the likelihood of error to a tolerable level.

It is often the case that two or more events occur which combine to create the risk. Nevertheless, aviation and air traffic control require a degree of human input and it would be naive to expect such a complex operation to exist without ever involving incidents. The best that can be achieved is that those occurrences result in a fail-safe rather than a fail-dangerous situation.

The perception of risk can mean different things to different people. A pilot flying an aircraft at high speed in busy airspace may well consider the close proximity of another aircraft to be a real threat. Careful analysis later, however, may reveal that safety was not compromised.

Less than one third of the reported Airproxes occur in controlled airspace. Most (70 per cent in 2007) take place in Class G airspace, and rarely involve civil air transport flights. In 2007, 20 Airproxes involved gliding sites.

For passenger-carrying flights in 2007, none of the reported Airproxes were assessed as Class A (risk bearing) and only 5 were assessed as Class B (safety was compromised). One of these occurred in Class D airspace; the other four were in Class G airspace. These were the lowest results recorded, both in numbers and when compared as a ratio to the increased number of hours flown.

Airproxes involving at least one military flight showed a similar trend with only two assessed as risk bearing – again, the lowest on record. Overall, the number reported in 2007 was 154, compared with a previous five-year average of 191.

Detailed painstaking and impartial investigation of such occurrences has to be available for the purpose of learning from the failings of humans, of machines and of working practices so that, where appropriate, modifications can be introduced in an attempt to eliminate similar situations in the future. The public notion of incidents in the air is described in the media by the emotive term 'near miss'. In fact, the correct description covers all Airprox incidents investigated by the UK Airprox Board.

The Board is an independent organisation sponsored jointly by the Civil Aviation Authority and the Ministry of Defence. There are eight civilian and six military members (all volunteers) and a chairman. Their expertise covers all aspects of civil and military aviation and air traffic control.

The sole objective of any investigation is to enhance flight safety by identifying the reasons for the incident and to take steps to ensure, as far as possible, that the situation does not occur again. It is not the purpose of the Board to apportion blame or liability; therefore the names of companies and individuals involved are not included in the reports. The individual reports, and the general trends, are freely available on the internet.

3. Control Centre Operations

UK airspace is currently managed from three Air Traffic Control centres. Two, at Swanwick and Manchester, are responsible for traffic in the London Flight Information Region, while the third, based at Prestwick, is responsible for traffic in the Scottish Flight Information Region and also the eastern half of the North Atlantic.

A replacement building has been completed at Prestwick, adjacent to the existing facilities, and when it becomes operational in 2010 it will result in the closure of Manchester and the realignment of the boundary between London and Scottish airspace to the south of its present position. This will be the final phase in the NATS strategy to operate from only two centres.

The Centres are as follows:
London Area Control Centre (LACC)
(Callsign **London**)

This is located at Swanwick, near Fareham in Hampshire, with responsibility for en route traffic throughout most of England and Wales and the surrounding sea areas.

This centre commenced operations on 27 January 2002, taking over responsibility for en route traffic in the London FIR, which had previously been managed from West Drayton. Swanwick is the world's largest control centre, handling traffic in some of the world's busiest and most complex airspace.

The move to Swanwick also introduced a new way of working. Instead of a team of tactical controllers dealing with each sector, the Swanwick operation involves a tactical controller and a dedicated planner controller who is able to resolve possible conflicts in advance, thereby reducing the tactical controllers' workload. The planner and tactical controllers have equal status and are qualified to work in both roles.

Around 350 civil controllers and 170 assistants work around the clock in shifts, or 'watches', usually in a pattern of four days on, then two days off. The rota system uses a variety of work periods, designed to match the traffic loadings which vary considerably

*Engineering Control Centre,
Swanwick, Hampshire NATS*

throughout the 24-hour day. At night, for example, many of the London sectors are relatively quiet whereas for the Oceanic Area Control Centre the early hours of the morning are particularly busy.

As well as managing en route traffic over England and Wales, Swanwick also has responsibility for flights in the Greater London area and the southeast of England up to FL245 which are arriving at and departing from the region's airports – Heathrow, Gatwick, Luton, Stansted, Farnborough, Biggin Hill and Northolt. This takes place from a dedicated operations room, where teams of controllers form the London Terminal Control Centre (LTCC), also using the callsign London. This unit moved out of the former West Drayton centre in November 2007.

The systems and procedures in use at Swanwick are very similar to those used at other centres, both in the UK and across Europe, although new and exciting ways of managing traffic are currently being developed and tested.

London Flight Information Service, Swanwick NATS

Manchester Area Control Centre (MACC)
(Callsign **Manchester**)

Located at Manchester Airport, with responsibility for traffic in the north of England up to and including FL285.

It is planned to close Manchester and transfer its operations to the new Scottish Centre when it opens in 2010.

Scottish Area Control Centre (SCATCC)
(Callsign **Scottish**)

Located near Prestwick Airport and responsible for traffic over Scotland, Northern Ireland and part of the North Sea.

The area covered by Scottish is the largest in Europe. This centre is being replaced by new facilities which are due to be ready in 2010.

Oceanic Area Control Centre (OACC)
(Callsign **Shanwick**)

Located near Prestwick Airport and responsible for flights over the eastern half of the North Atlantic. Full details of its operation can be found in the chapter covering the North Atlantic.

Control Centre, Swanwick NATS

Operations Room, Swanwick NATS

Controllers at Maastricht
EUROCONTROL

Shannon Air Traffic Control Centre, Shannon (Callsign **Shannon**)

Located near Shannon Airport and responsible for traffic in the Republic of Ireland. This centre is the responsibility of the Irish Aviation Authority.

Maastricht Upper Area Control Centre, Maastricht (Callsign **Maastricht**)

Located near Maastricht-Aaachen Airport in the Netherlands and responsible for traffic above FL245 in Belgium, the Netherlands, Luxembourg and the northwest of Germany.

Opened in 1972 as the prototype for the Functonal Airspace Blocks, which are being planned across Europe, it handles around 1.5 million flights a year using state-of-the art systems.

Operating principles

Most of the flights handled by controllers at the area control centres operate in controlled airspace, either in the airways or in upper airspace. However, non-radar services to aircraft outside controlled airspace are also provided, as well as the Distress and Diversion service for aircraft requiring assistance.

Each flight information region is divided into a system of geographical areas, known as sectors, and traffic within each sector is the responsibility of a team of controllers, usually employing one or two dedicated radio frequencies for communication.

Each sector is designed to give the most efficient management of the traffic flows; therefore they vary considerably in extent, according to the number of flights which can normally be expected, and their phases of flight. For example, a sector which normally only handles high-flying en route traffic will usually be much larger than a busy sector dealing with a large number of climbing and descending traffic. In each case, daily predictions of traffic flows determine the capacity for each sector.

Throughout Europe, the management of traffic flows is achieved through the processing of flight plans by the Central Flow Management Unit at EUROCONTROL, which was set up in 1996 in order to address the serious problem of delay across the region – some 20 per cent of flights were regularly being delayed by 30 minutes.

The Central Flow Management Unit of Eurocontrol Eurocontrol

Dealing with fluctuations in demand is still a tactical requirement at the centres, and traffic planners often have to re-route some flights through a quieter sector or implement flow restrictions to temporarily limit the number of flights. During quiet periods (for example, at night) it is common for two or even three sectors to be combined into one, using a single radio frequency for the whole area.

In many parts of the UK, sectors are divided vertically, with one team of controllers handling traffic at lower levels while their colleagues manage flights at high level, each team being on different radio frequencies. In busy airspace, as in the London area, there may be as many as four separate sectors, one above the other.

However, simply dividing the airspace into smaller and smaller sectors in order to meet increasing traffic levels creates its own problems. Firstly, pilots have to change radio frequencies more often, taking up precious radio time and increasing the possibility of mistakes; secondly, the co-ordination process required as flights transfer from one sector to the next increases the workload for controllers.

Other methods of meeting the demand need to be developed, and many technological advances are being made which will enable this to be achieved.

One existing method of reducing the need for co-ordination between sectors is to have a system of 'standing agreements'. These arrangements mean that an agreement is established between two sectors so that flights arriving into the sector from a particular direction will always enter at an agreed point and flight level. No advance co-ordination between the two sectors is required unless for some reason the agreed criteria are not going to be achieved.

Most of the sectors operate within the standing agreement system.

Radar Control

This involves the provision of a control service to aircraft using information derived from radar. It is mandatory for flights using the airways, the upper airspace or Class A terminal airspace. Most civil passenger and freight-carrying aircraft in UK airspace route under the surveillance of area radar control. Military traffic using the airways or upper air routes also comes within the jurisdiction of the civil Air Traffic Control system.

Airways and Upper Air Routes

The airways system applies below FL245, with a defined width of 10 nm or more. Virtually all airways are Class A airspace up to FL195, and Class C between FL195 and FL245.

Flights may operate in an airway only if a flight plan has been filed, the aircraft has certain equipment on board and the flight is being conducted under IFR.

Above FL245, in the Upper Airspace Control Area (Class C airspace), airways are replaced by Upper Air Traffic Service Routes, with no defined width, although for air traffic purposes they are deemed to be 10 nm wide. Although often referred to as airways, Upper ATS routes are simply straight lines between radio navigation beacons (Very High Frequency Omnidirectional Radio or VORs) or geographical positions, known as Name Code Designators.

These are points, defined by their respective latitudes and longitudes, which have no supporting facilities on the ground. They all have five letters, and are always quoted in upper case letters. Some have names which relate to a local landmark or town, but many are selected at random. They normally indicate positions where routes intersect, at changes in base levels of airways (in lower airspace) or on international boundaries.

Some airways and upper air traffic service routes are known as Conditional Routes because they are not always available for planning flights. There are three categories of Conditional Routes with different conditions applicable to their use.

Most long-distance routes in the UK are designated as Area Navigation (RNAV) routes where the carriage of certain navigation equipment is compulsory.

Because aircraft above FL245 are under control, the controllers can often clear pilots to route directly between distant positions which may take the flight many miles away from the routes shown on aeronautical charts. The implementation of long-range area navigation systems, employing satellite technology and on-board navigation equipment, enables flights to follow precise routes without reference to ground-based facilities.

The Use of Radar

Primary radar relies on the reflected signal from a 'target' – for example, an aircraft – which is received by a radar antenna and displayed on the controller's radar screen. Primary radar is limited by the quality of the information received and by the strength of the original signal from the ground-based transmitter. Obviously, the greater the distance between the transmitter and the aircraft, the weaker the reflection will be.

Radar Station at Great Dunn Fell NATS

Even with a good signal, positively determining the location and altitude of an aircraft is difficult for a number of reasons, and managing today's traffic environment would simply not be possible without a more accurate and reliable means of identification.

Secondary surveillance radar, however, differs from primary radar in that a signal containing specific information is transmitted from special equipment (a transponder) on the aircraft. This signal is picked up by the ground-based radar and converted into legible information before being displayed on the controller's screen.

The system was first developed during World War 2 as a means of identifying friendly aircraft and was known as IFF – Identification Friend or Foe.

A radio signal transmitted from the ground was received by equipment on the aircraft and recognised as being 'friendly', in which case a coded reply was returned, providing the ground unit with confirmation that the approaching aircraft was one of its own. A hostile aircraft would be unable to reply, thereby alerting the operator to the possibility of attack.

The system in use today is, of course, far more sophisticated but the principle is the same. The radar sends out signals 'interrogating' all the transponders in range, processes the information received and then displays the details on the radar screen.

In addition, while primary radar displays only the position of the aircraft target, modern secondary radar is capable of interrogating the various systems on the flightdeck and having those details presented to the controller. For example, the controller is able to check that the cleared flight level selected by the pilot is in fact the correct one.

The simplest type of transponder (Mode A) uses a four-digit code, allocated by the controller and entered into the transponder by the pilot. This code, known as a squawk, can be observed by the controller on his display, providing him with positive identification.

Aircraft flying in Class A or Class C airspace must be operating a transponder which has an additional facility, Mode C (or Mode Charlie), which can be interrogated to provide the controller with more detail.

A flight plan has to be submitted to Air Traffic Control before an aircraft can fly in controlled airspace. This plan gives detailed information on the routeing, aircraft type, callsign and so on and, when approved, the flight will be allocated a four-figure squawk code.

Most of the airlines provide scheduled service details weeks or months in advance, and the information is stored in the Central Flow Management Unit at EUROCONTROL until the day of the flight.

Squawk codes consist of the numbers 0 to 7, meaning that there is a theoretical total of 4096 codes available for use. In fact, many squawks are reserved for particular situations so the available number is actually far less. With daily European traffic figures now in the region of 30,000, each code has to be reissued ten or more times each day. This is creating significant logistical problems for the computer systems, and misreading of information by the radar equipment is on the increase. A more reliable system is already in use by many major airlines.

Immediately prior to departure, the pilot will enter the squawk code allocated by ATC as part of the clearance message. As the aircraft climbs away from the airport, the squawk code will be picked up by the area radar and processed though computers at the ATC centre, matching the code with the flight details. The 'label' which appears on the controller's display will show its identity, altitude, cleared flight level, destination and attitude (climbing or descending).

Occasionally, for identification purposes, the pilot may be asked to squawk ident, by operating a switch on the transponder which causes the particular radar return to increase in intensity or to flash on the screen.

Squawk codes can be used for several other situations to provide ATC with invaluable information on the progress of the flight. Code 7700, for example, is the code used to denote an emergency on-board. Code 7600 indicates radio failure, while Code 7500 warns the controller of some unlawful interference with the flight.

Other codes have been introduced which are used to indicate the types of flight and their intentions. For example, flights in receipt of a service from London Information will be requested to squawk 1177.

General aviation flights operating within five nm of certain areas of controlled airspace should tune their radios to the local control frequency and then squawk a specific code which indicates to ATC that they are 'listening out' in case the controller wishes to make contact.

The frequencies and listening out squawks are:
- Manchester Approach 118.575 (7366)
- Luton Radar 129.550 (0013)
- Essex Radar 120.625 (0013)
- London City 126.825 (0012)
- Gatwick Approach 132.700 (0012)

The squawk of 7000, known as the 'conspicuity code', is used by aircraft – usually general aviation (GA) flights – which are operating outside controlled airspace and not in receipt of any type of service.

Flights which are receiving a service from a local airfield may be allocated a squawk code which indicates to other controllers the unit in communication with the aircraft. Newcastle Approach, for example, may use squawk codes from 3720 to 3766 for aircraft under its jurisdiction.

Aircraft with radio problems may be asked by ATC to squawk ident if the transmissions are being received, thus indicating to the ground that radio reception is functioning, even if the transmitter on the aircraft is not.

One important safety feature of the transponder is the detection of the actual level being flown. If the pressure subscale on the altimeter has been set incorrectly the controller will be able to observe that the aircraft's actual level varies from the cleared level. A number of potentially dangerous incidents have been avoided through the use of this facility.

Separation Standards
The prime responsibility of the air traffic controller is the safety of flights under his control; in part, the means of ensuring safety relies on making sure that the flights under control are kept apart by internationally agreed minimum distances, known as Separation Standards.

The degree of control varies according to the type of airspace but, in general, where the flights are in controlled airspace ATC is responsible for their separation. Outside controlled airspace the pilot is always responsible for remaining clear of other traffic and terrain clearance, even though he may be receiving some kind of control service.

Standard vertical or horizontal separation is to be provided, except when specified otherwise, between the following:

- All flights in Class A or Class B airspace
- Flights operating under IFR in Class C, D and E airspace
- Flights operating under IFR and VFR in Class C airspace
- Flights operating under IFR and Special VFR
- Flights operating under Special VFR
- Participating flights operating under IFR in Class F airspace
- Flights operating under IFR in Class G airspace, provided they are in receipt of a service from approach controllers.

My Travel A321 – 211 Shaun Grist

If the controller considers it necessary, or if the pilot requests it, the separation minima may be increased.

The opposite can also apply. Separation may be reduced in some cases, for example in the vicinity of an airport, when both aircraft can be seen by the controller, or if the pilot of each aircraft can see the other aircraft and can maintain safe separation. On Advisory Routes, the minimum vertical separation of 500ft applies in accordance with the Quadrantal Rule.

Separation of aircraft can be achieved by one of two methods: Vertical Separation and Horizontal Separation.

Vertical Separation

This is where the vertical distance between civilian aircraft operating in controlled airspace is never less than the following minima:

- Up to FL290 – 1,000ft
- Above FL290 – 1,000ft, except that where an aircraft is not approved for RVSM flight the separation from other flights shall be increased to 2,000ft.

Radar Consoles, Swanwick NATS

Horizontal Separation
Separation between aircraft varies considerably depending on available ground facilities, the position of aircraft and other circumstances; therefore only a summary of the principles is given here.

There are three types of horizontal separation:
- Lateral separation based on specified tracks or geographical positions
- Longitudinal separation based on time and distance
- Separation based on the use of radar or other surveillance system.

Lateral Separation based on specified tracks
Lateral separation applies where the distance between aircraft is never less than specified, according to the conditions. These conditions vary between 15 and 30 nm, according to the tracks of the aircraft and their respective distances from radio navigation aids.

Lateral Separation based on geographical positions
Geographical separation must be positively indicated by position reports over different locations, which are specified in the relevant documents as being adequately separated. The separation distance must be constant or increasing.

Longitudinal Separation based on time and distance
This is arranged to ensure that aircraft spacing is never less than the minimum required. For this purpose the controller may require flights to depart from an airfield at specified intervals, to increase or reduce speed to maintain separation, or to hold a following flight over a specific location in order to lose time.

Separation by time varies, according to different circumstances, between two minutes and ten minutes. The longitudinal separation based on distance also varies considerably, but can be reduced to five nm in certain circumstances.

Radar Separation
Horizontal separation using radar applies to most flights using controlled airspace. The separation may be as low as 3 miles, when both aircraft are operating in lower airspace, and when authorised by the CAA. In most cases, the minimum is 5 miles, but in some situations it must be increased to ten miles.

Terminal Manoeuvring Areas (TMAs)
In UK airspace there are Terminal Areas at London, Manchester, Belfast, and in Scotland the Scottish Terminal Area contains airports at Prestwick, Glasgow and Edinburgh. The Terminal Control function provides a dedicated approach service to aircraft arriving at airports within its boundaries and also directs departing traffic into the airways system.

The London TMA unit moved from West Drayton to Swanwick in November 2007. Its workstations are divided into North, South, East, Midlands and Capital. The Capital sector deals with traffic between FL175 and

FL215, and extends out to the boundaries with France, Belgium and the Netherlands, meaning that traffic is handed over directly to one of the continental sectors.

Controllers work in pairs, one co-ordinating the entry of flights towards the holding points, the other monitoring the flights in the holding stacks and sending them on to the final approach. They also keep an eye on what their colleague is doing so that possible problems are spotted before they develop. A similar system operates for departures.

TMA airspace is complex and busy, the London TMA being the busiest in the world in terms of the number of flights per square kilometre. The London TMA has a number of subdivisions with differing lower levels, most of which are around 5,000ft. Due to its complexity the problem of unauthorised infringements by general aviation flights is increasing and can be extremely disruptive to the regular traffic flows approaching the airports.

In order to reduce the number of aircraft straying into the London TMA, special software has been designed and implemented to assist controllers in identifying such aircraft in time for corrective action to be taken.

The system – the Controlled Airspace Infringement Tool (CAIT) – uses an electronic map of the terminal airspace, which is built into the software, covering not just the plan area but also the various levels. If an unauthorised flight crosses the boundary into the controlled area the data block turns magenta, alerting the controller to the problem. Without this facility, these flights are very difficult to spot, especially when workload is high.

Radar Controllers, Swanwick
NATS

Military ATC

At Swanwick, military Air Traffic Control staff work alongside civilian colleagues in the main operations room, providing a service which ensures the safe and expeditious integration of military aircraft through the civil airways system. Known as the London Joint Area Organisation (LJAO), military controllers also provide a service to civilian aircraft that wish to transit outside of the airways.

The LJAO areas of responsibility are divided into North West, West, South West, Central and South East. A separate unit has responsibility for the eastern side of the country.

Under the Flexible Use of Airspace (FUA) policy, military and civil controllers work together to make the best use of the UK's limited airspace resource to increase the capacity of the ATC system.

Since military traffic is often required to cross airways, the most frequently used crossings have been established as either Airways Crossing Slots or Radar Video Corridors, at specified levels and widths. Pilots still need to contact London or Scottish Military Radar prior to the crossing, but the procedure is simplified by the fact that these blocks of airspace have been established for the specific purpose of facilitating the penetration of controlled airspace.

An alternative procedure is now in operation at Swanwick, designed to allow the passage of fast jets through the airways system with the minimum of co-ordination between controllers. After departure from his base station, the pilot requests a crossing clearance. The controller selects a box on his radar screen, and enters the navigation points for the route requested by the pilot, together with the flight levels, at least 5 minutes before the planned entry time.

This box automatically appears on each of the civil controllers' screens affected by the requested route, and a pink dotted line appears across the controlled airspace, indicating the proposed track. The civil controller checks the route and the requested flight levels, and if acceptable, enters a tick on his screen alongside each part of the route. If the proposed route is unacceptable, the controller enters a cross together with a suggested change of level.

In most cases these requests are granted, as five minutes gives the controller plenty of time to ensure his traffic avoids the jets. Once agreed, the dotted track turns solid and the jets are cleared to cross. The civil controller indicates this on his board by a pink crossing strip.

The benefit of this system is that it is fully automatic – no discussion between the controllers is necessary.

Military controllers are also permitted to arrange crossings of airways without prior co-ordination, but they are responsible for keeping their aircraft five miles away from any civil traffic or 5,000ft above or below.

Military Low Flying

The UK military low flying system covers most airspace from the surface to 2,000ft. Built-up areas, controlled airspace, air traffic zones, and so on are avoided. Many of the routes are used in one direction only during daylight.

In Scotland, the Highlands Restricted Area provides for special military training in Instrument Meteorological Conditions and is therefore closed to other traffic. In tactical training areas military jets may fly as low as 100ft above the surface. They operate on the 'see and avoid principle' since radar cover is generally not possible.

Civilian pilots who wish to operate at low level are encouraged to notify the military authorities through the Civil Aviation Notification Procedure (CANP) so that military flights can avoid the area. Details of locations and times are passed to military briefing units prior to flight planning.

The general advice to civil pilots is to fly higher than 2,000ft above ground level wherever possible; to avoid the height band between 250ft and 1,000ft; and to keep a good lookout at all times.

Opposite page
Transaero B747 – 219B
Shaun Grist

4. Airport Procedures

Airport capacity across Europe continues to be a limiting factor in the ever-rising demand for more flights, with increasing delays, additional costs and more pollution for the airlines.

The number of flights in European airspace is expected to double by 2015 (compared with 2008), while in the developing world, traffic in China and India has increased by as much as a third each year. Providing additional runways and their associated infrastructure is a lengthy process, both at political and environmental levels, and all the forecasts show that traffic growth will outstrip capacity at many of Europe's airports.

In the UK, the government has already given approval to the building of additional runways at Heathrow and Stansted, amid storms of protest from the local population and environmentalists, so it will probably be several years before these become a reality – even longer if the threatened legal challenges succeed.

At EUROCONTROL, therefore, the focus has been on improving the efficiency of existing facilities, evaluating the potential for releasing latent capacity and maximising best practice. ACE (the Airport Airside Capacity Analysis, Enhancement and Planning process) has shown that in many cases an improvement of 20 per cent can be achieved at peak times. However, even with an anticipated 60 per cent increase in airport capacity by 2025, EUROCONTROL forecasts anticipate that the system will be unable to handle 3.5 million flights each year.

Runway incursions

Unauthorised incursions onto runways and taxiways continue to be a major concern, highlighting the need for continued research and technological development. In many cases, simple errors and misunderstandings are to blame.

Safety nets – for example, the Surface Movement Guidance and Control System at Heathrow and Gatwick – give airport users moving map displays through the use of selective transponder transmissions, issuing

Air China Boeing 747 - 4J6 Air China Airlines

automatic warnings to pilots, drivers and controllers when approaching an active runway or when a possible conflict is detected.

Even so, human factors are a significant element, and part of the reason why the problem cannot be solved by technology alone.

Airports and airfields

Airport operations vary considerably depending on the volume of traffic and the type of aircraft. A major airport such as London Heathrow needs complex air traffic management and control systems in order to cope safely with large numbers of arrivals and departures. On the other hand, small landing strips used by general aviation and gliders often operate with the simplest of procedures.

The airspace around airports and small airfields is directly related to the traffic volume. Obviously, somewhere like Heathrow needs to be fully protected from unknown and unauthorised aircraft, and for this reason, it benefits from being in Class A airspace. Smaller airports may be in Class D airspace, allowing their use by a mix of general aviation flights and commercial airliners, while small gliding sites and landing strips will usually be in Class G airspace.

Large-scale operations demand suitably designed Air Traffic Control procedures, with the responsibility for the various elements subdivided among a number of control staff.

Aerodrome Traffic Zones, Control Zones and Control Areas

Many UK airfields have an area of protected airspace where local Air Traffic Control rules are applied. These vary according to individual requirements and full details are published in the UK Integrated Aeronautical Information Package which is freely available on the internet.

Typically, the protected airspace at civil airfields consists of Aerodrome Traffic Zones (ATZ), Control Zones (CTR) and Control Areas (CTA).

The Aerodrome Traffic Zone is a column of controlled airspace, five nm in diameter, centred on the longest notified runway, extending from the aerodrome surface up to 2,500ft.

The Control Zone is also a column of airspace, typically ten nm in diameter, centred on the longest notified runway, extending from the aerodrome surface up to a specified upper limit – for example, FL105 (approximately 10,500ft).

The Control Area is an additional area of regulated airspace which extends beyond the zone. Its upper limit is the same as the zone (FL105 in this example) but the lower limit is variable, often in steps to facilitate arriving and departing flights. A Control Area is usually oval in shape, perhaps 20 nm at its longest point and 10 nm across at its narrowest (the same as the Zone).

Depending on the surrounding airspace structure, the Control Areas may be merged with those of other airfields. The longest axis of the oval shape coincides with the airfield runway headings, providing protection for arriving and departing aircraft.

Control Areas and Zones may be Class A, D or E to suit local circumstances.

High-powered surveillance system at London Heathrow that tracks aircraft and vehicles on the ground and presents a radar display to controllers Author

At military airfields a similar system is used, known as Military Aerodrome Traffic Zones (MATZ) with an extended portion of airspace on the runway heading, known as a stub. Aircraft must not enter the Control Area or Zone unless authorised to do so by the airfield controller, but they may be flown outside the controlled airspace without necessarily talking to the local ATC unit.

Flights outside Controlled Airspace

Most airfields provide a service to traffic passing through their general area, in addition, of course, to those flights wishing to actually land or depart. A number of civil and military units take part in the Lower Airspace Radar Service (LARS) providing a service to aircraft in transit through their region.

The level of service offered by individual airfields will vary from time to time according to the controllers' workload, the distance of the aircraft from the airfield and the kind of service requested by the pilot based on the flight conditions under which the aircraft is operating.

A range of air traffic services are available to flights operating outside controlled airspace (as explained in detail in Chapter 2), but they are limited to the extent that not all aircraft in the area are necessarily talking to a controller. Pilots of these aircraft are responsible at all times for collision avoidance and terrain clearance.

At many of the smaller airports, controllers have to handle a mix of large passenger jets and small light aircraft. Many of the small general aviation aircraft using local airfields will be operating under Visual Flight Rules, and their pilots may well not be qualified to fly under Instrument Flight Rules; therefore controllers will be unable to instruct pilots to make turns or changes of level which might take them into cloud.

Of course, if an airport is within Class A airspace, visual flight is not permitted, except that in some cases (as in the London area) special traffic lanes are available where certain flights are permitted to fly under Special VFR.

ATC Simulator for the new Control Tower at Heathrow *Micronav Ltd*

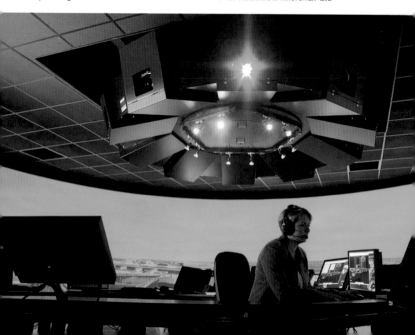

Visual Reference Points

At selected locations around most airfields a number of Visual Reference Points (VRPs) exist for the guidance of pilots operating under Visual Flight Rules. The VRPs are chosen because of their proximity to prominent features on the ground, which can be easily identified from the air – for example, lakes, reservoirs, motorway intersections, bridges, power stations, television masts, and so on. Each VRP is also located by reference to its bearing and distance from a radio navigation beacon in the vicinity so that suitably equipped aircraft can cross-check their position.

Pilots operating under VFR will usually be required to route via one of the Visual Reference Points, and, if necessary, to hold at that position while awaiting permission to enter controlled airspace.

Use of Transponders

The majority of general aviation aircraft flying outside regulated airspace are fitted with a special transmitter which broadcasts a four-digit number, called a squawk. The transmission is detected by radar and displayed to the controller on radar, thereby providing an identification of an individual flight. The use of a transponder is mandatory in the Scottish FIR above 6,000ft, and in the London FIR above FL100.

Most civil and military airfields are allocated a number of dedicated squawk codes specifically for their use, enabling controllers to identify the ATC unit currently dealing with the flight. They are allocated at random to light aircraft in their region area so that the aircraft position can be detected by secondary radar and indicated on radar screens at adjacent ATC units. Controllers are therefore able to tell which particular air traffic unit is handling an aircraft which appears on radar.

Where an aircraft is outside unregulated airspace and not in receipt of an ATC service, the pilot will set a squawk of 7000 on the transponder. This is a nationally recognised 'conspicuity code' which tells controllers that the flight is not receiving a service from ATC.

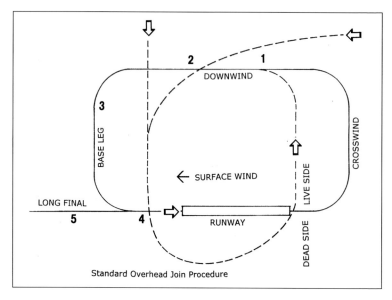

2

1

DOWNWIND

3

BASE LEG

CROSSWIND

← SURFACE WIND

LIVE SIDE

LONG FINAL

5   4

RUNWAY

DEAD SIDE

Standard Overhead Join Procedure

Airfields

Aircraft operating around airfields must comply with a series of standard procedures, shown in the diagram, although large and busy airports will be governed by their own special rules. A left-hand circuit is shown, where all turns are to the left; a right-hand pattern would be one where turns are to the right.

It is standard practice to operate a left-hand circuit unless Air Traffic Control instructs otherwise. In fact, left-hand circuits will not be referred to by ATC, whereas a right-hand circuit will be specified.

The Visual Traffic Circuit

Around each airfield a pattern exists which all flights must follow, unless directed otherwise by ATC. Non-radio traffic also fly the same pattern, known as the visual circuit. The area to the left of the centreline of the runway is known as the live side; the area to the right is the dead side.

Flights which are unable to carry out a straight-in approach will be instructed to enter the circuit by flying downwind – that is, in the opposite direction, and parallel to, the

Visual Traffic Circuit

landing runway and some distance to one side. The pilot will report '*downwind*' when abeam the upwind end of the runway (1), or '*late downwind*' if the aircraft has passed the downwind end of the runway (2).

When the aircraft has passed abeam the end of the runway, at a distance no greater than four miles, it will turn to the left onto the base leg which is at right-angles to the runway heading (3).

As the aircraft reaches the extended centreline of the runway it is turned left again onto the final approach, in line with the runway, in preparation for landing (4).

An aircraft making a straight-in approach to the runway in use may be cleared to fly along the runway heading on a 'long final' approach, which is between four and eight miles from the runway (5).

The track between the upwind end of the runway and the downwind leg is known as the cross-wind leg.

Training flights often operate from the smaller airfields, and 'flying the circuit' is common for this purpose. Many flights will not actually land and stop; they will 'touch and go', meaning that the aircraft will land, continue along the runway for a short distance, and then take off again.

Pilots wishing to join the traffic circuit at an airfield, unless instructed otherwise, will carry out a Standard Overhead Join Procedure, under which the aircraft is flown at 2,000ft from the live side and to the right of the touch-down end of the runway (reporting 'overhead'), descending in a left-hand turn to cross the upwind end of the runway at 1,000ft, and then to join the downwind leg of the traffic circuit.

Procedural Flights

In poor visibility, at airfields without radar, or where an existing radar unit is unserviceable, aircraft may make an approach to determine the position of the landing runway by making a 'procedural approach'. This involves positioning the aircraft over a low-powered Non-Directional Radio Beacon (NDB) alongside the runway.

Depending on local requirements, the aircraft is flown to a position overhead the beacon at a specified level, perhaps 2,500ft. When at the beacon, the aircraft is turned onto a specified heading which takes it away from the airfield, at an angle of 45 degrees to the runway heading. After flying on this heading for one minute, a 180-degree turn is made to bring the aircraft onto a reciprocal track; a 45-degree turn is then made to position the aircraft in line with the landing runway.

At this point, the pilot commences the descent on the runway centreline and will continue to descend until the airfield decision height is reached. If the runway is not then visible to the pilot, the aircraft must be flown along the runway centreline in the 'missed approach procedure'. The aircraft will then continue on the runway heading, climbing to a specified level, then returning to the NDB for another attempt.

This kind of exercise is often practised at airfields around the country by both military and civilian pilots while undergoing training.

Virgin Atlantic B747 – 41R Shaun Grist

Standard Departures and Arrivals

Special routes for departing and arriving flights are in operation at most UK airports. These are known as SIDs (Standard Instrument Departures) or STARs (Standard Arrival Routes). These are designed to facilitate departures and arrivals so that ATC involvement is minimised, since the route will provide the pilot with all the information needed to follow a safe course. Flight Management Systems are programmed with the various headings and levels so that many aircraft are capable of following the required routes automatically.

Precision Area Navigation (P-RNAV) in terminal airspace enables certified aircraft to navigate independently of any ground-based radio aids, using navigational systems on the flightdeck which allow the aircraft to follow a predetermined series of waypoints which are loaded into a database.

Flight Plans

For any flight which is to operate in controlled airspace, a flight plan must be filed detailing various aspects of the proposed flight. For flights which will route through European airspace, the plan must be filed with the Central Flow Management Unit (CFMU) of EUROCONTROL, at one of two processing centres in Haren and Bretigny.

The CFMU is an operational unit of EUROCONTROL, and its function is to enhance safety across Europe through the co-ordinated management of the air traffic. It ensures that available capacity is used effectively and that congestion is avoided.

Co-ordination with the CFMU is maintained through a Flow Management Position at every European ATC centre, playing an important role in notifying CFMU of local issues, such as staffing problems, workload and technical matters.

For the airlines, most flight plans are filed months in advance of the day of the flight, especially for scheduled services which will be known well in advance. The whole process is run automatically, checking for errors, and plans which contain incorrect or unacceptable elements are not approved.

The plans are handled through three phases – Strategic, covering a period of several months to a couple of days before the flight, when overall traffic predictions are prepared, followed by the Pre-Tactical level, covering the two days before the flight, where action is taken to fine tune the air traffic system, and finally the Tactical level, on the day of the flight, where air traffic flow management adjustments are made.

When the final approval for the flight is issued by the CFMU, it may include a departure slot time which is based on the aircraft's Calculated Take-off Time (CTOT). As European airspace becomes more congested, an increasing number of airports are often subject to flow restrictions. It is important that the departure controller and the aircraft operator appreciate the importance of complying with slot times so as to prevent bottlenecks in the system and controller overload. Normally, a slot time means that the flight must depart within a tolerance of 15 minutes, being five minutes before or ten minutes after the slot. If for any reason this cannot be complied with, a new flight plan has to be filed.

Electronic Flight Progress Strips on a display by Frequentis NATS

PENIL / MALUD / WAL				
MALUD 2047	290L ↑	**RYR288** RYANAIR	BDW EGSS UL975 UL10	**LIFFY** 2039
	230	M B738		310
PENIL 2058	300	**RYR341** RYANAIR	EGGW BDW UL28 UL70 UV14	**MCT** 2051
		M B738 T450		
PENIL 2058	290	**MAH622** MALEV	LHBP BDW UL26 UL70 UV14	**MAMUL** 2045
		M B738 T450		
PENIL 2059	300 240	**BCY155T** CITYIRELAND	EGLC EGAC N601 P6 L28 L10	**ASHIP** 2053 240
		D328 T320		
PENIL 2100	290	**RYR293** RYANAIR	EGSS BDW UL28 UL70 UV14	**MCT** 2052 300
		M B738 T450		
PENIL 2100	280	**BCY5121** CITYIRELAND	EGLC BDW N601 P6 L28 L708	**ASHIP** 2056 240
		M RJ85 280		200
MALUD 2101	230	**TAY14F** QUALITY	EGAA EGNX ROK1E	**KELLY** 2055
		H A30B T460		
PENIL 2101	300 200	**BEE338X** JERSEY	EGHK EGNS N601 P6 L28 L10	**WAL** 2055 240
		S DH8D T355		
Point		Open	To	Multi-

Most UK airports still use a paper flight progress strip for each flight, providing controllers with details of the aircraft type, callsign, route, speed, et cetera, although the major airports are gradually moving to electronic strips.

The strips, which are automatically generated by the system some 15 minutes prior to the flight arriving at the sector boundary, are arranged in front of the controller, either in a rack or on a screen, in the order in which they will arrive, colour coded as departures or arrivals. Blue strips indicate departures; brown strips indicate arrivals. As the controller issues an instruction, the details are either written on the strip or displayed electronically on a screen.

Stansted switched over to electronic strips late in 2004, the first UK airport to abandon the paper method, and Heathrow also did away with paper strips when the new control tower was commissioned in 2007. Many countries now operate this system, and paper strips will eventually disappear. One significant advantage is the ability to share information electronically with other controllers, something which is not possible with paper strips and handwritten notes.

The new Control Tower at London Heathrow Author

Arrivals

Flights routeing to an airport are first transferred to the airport approach frequency by controllers at the control centre. Information about the airport and local weather conditions can be obtained from the recorded Automatic Terminal Information Service or directly from the airport controllers.

Traffic may follow a Standard Arrival Route, or alternatively will be 'vectored' to a position which places it in line with the landing runway, after which the aircraft will lock on to the Instrument Landing System (ILS). At small airfields where ILS is not available, a visual approach may be possible, or alternatively a surveillance radar approach will be provided by approach control.

An additional method for general aviation flights involves the Global Positioning System (GPS), which has been authorised for arrivals for general aviation flights, following successful trials at Shoreham, Gloucestershire, Inverness, Exeter, Durham Tees Valley and Blackpool.

Runways

Each runway at an airport is identified according to its compass bearing, rounded off to the nearest 10 degrees, with the final zero omitted. For example, if the centreline of the runway faces 266 degrees in one direction and 86 degrees in the opposite direction, the runway will be designated as 27 or 09, depending on the direction of the landing and departing traffic.

At Heathrow the two parallel runways are described as 'left' and 'right' respectively as viewed from the flightdeck. An 'active' runway is one which is being used for arrivals and departures.

Before 2 July 1987 the two main runways at Heathrow were designated as 28 and 10, but because of small annual changes in the magnetic bearing of the North Pole, the runway directions are now closer to 270 degrees/090 degrees than 280 degrees/010 degrees.

British Airways B747 landing on 09L at London Heathrow
Author

Manchester's runways were also changed early in 2009, from 06/24 to 05/23.

The Instrument Landing System provides assistance in guiding aircraft to the runway in all weather conditions. It uses two radio transmissions: the 'localizer', which indicates the centreline of the runway; and the 'glide path', a horizontal beam angled upwards at 3 degrees to provide the correct angle of approach.

Holding

Where airport conditions dictate – for example, traffic congestion, poor visibility, closed runways, and so on – arriving aircraft may be required to delay their approach by flying in a racetrack pattern, known as 'holding'. Where substantial delays are anticipated, aircraft may be held at high level many miles from the airport, sometimes for an hour or more, until they are able to make an approach to the airport.

Alternatively, it may be necessary for some flights to divert to an alternative airport, especially if the aircraft is low on fuel.

Holding patterns near airports are sometimes referred to as stacks because aircraft are stacked one above the other with 1,000ft separation between them. As the flight at the lowest level is cleared to leave the hold, other flights are 'laddered' down in 1,000ft increments. Flights which are required to hold will be requested, for example, to 'Enter the hold at Ockham, flight level nine zero, five minutes delay'. Full details of holding patterns are given on arrival charts for individual airfields.

If the expected delay is less than 20 minutes, the pilot will not usually be informed. Where the delay is longer, pilots will be given an indication of the length of time they can expect to hold and they will also be given an Expected Approach Time (EAT), which is the time the flight will be cleared to leave the holding stack to commence an approach. If the usual arrival stack is particularly congested, a flight may be rerouted to a less busy holding point to minimise the delay.

Categories I, II and III

Airports provided with an ILS conform to one of three categories enabling suitably equipped aircraft to land in varying degrees of poor visibility.

Airfields have various categories for approaching flights allocated to the different runways; basically these are in accordance with the following rules:

Category I (Cat I) Operation

A precision instrument approach and landing with a decision height not lower than 200ft and with either a visibility not less than 800 metres or a runway visual range of not less than 550 metres.

Category II (Cat II) Operation

A precision instrument approach and landing with a decision height lower than 200ft, but not lower than 100ft, and a runway visual range not less than 350 metres.

Category IIIA (Cat IIIA) Operation

A precision instrument approach and landing with either a decision height lower than 100ft or with no decision height and a runway visual range not less than 200 metres.

Category IIIB (Cat IIIB) Operation

A precision instrument approach and landing with either a decision height lower than 50ft or with no decision height and a runway visual range less than 200 metres but not less than 50 metres.

Category IIIC (Cat IIIC) Operation

A precision instrument approach and landing with no decision height and no runway visual range limitations.

During Cat II and Cat III operations, special Low Visibility Procedures have to be implemented to ensure that there is no adverse effect on the instrument landing system signals. Usually this means that the holding positions for departing aircraft are further back from the runway than otherwise, and also aircraft clearing the runway need to be at greater distances before reporting that they have vacated. Special lighting and marker boards are positioned at the holding points and at runway exits to indicate the limits of the sensitive areas.

Microwave Landing Systems

The system used at Heathrow for aircraft on final approach is the Microwave Landing System. This operates on frequencies around 5 GHz which are virtually free from interference. The system also has the advantage of allowing aircraft to lock on to the final approach anywhere within a 25-mile segment. In other words, aircraft can fly a curved approach instead of a straight-line approach as with ILS.

Heathrow became the first airport in the world to introduce MLS in 2004.

High Intensity Runway Operations (HIRO)

At busy airports, there is constant pressure to improve performance so that the most efficient use is made of the runways, taxiways and parking stands. At Heathrow, for example, already operating at its maximum capacity, even minor changes in procedures can make a difference, although safety is always the first priority.

Under the HIRO system, an aircraft on final approach may be given clearance to land if the preceding aircraft is still on the runway but is at least 2,500 metres from the touchdown point when the landing aircraft crosses the threshold.

Pilots of approaching aircraft need to ensure that they plan their landing procedures in order to achieve a minimum runway occupancy time so that the maximum landing rates can be maintained. The planned exit should be identified, together with the correct rate of deceleration, so that the aircraft can exit the runway as quickly as possible. Significant improvements to Runway Occupancy Times (ROTs) can be made by more efficient planning of exit procedures.

Departing aircraft occupancy times can also be improved if the aircraft is able to take off without delay. Research has shown that when an aircraft is holding on the runway there can be a delay in reacting to the controller's instruction to take off by as much

as 30 seconds. Reducing these delays would allow an additional two departures per hour.

Procedures to reduce ROTs are being introduced at airports across Europe with High Intensity Runway Operations (HIRO). Airlines need to decide on accurate and realistic occupancy times for the runways at each airport to be specified and supplied to the controlling authorities to enable them to optimise their approach procedures.

As an additional aid for improved efficiency, the Final Approach Spacing Tool (FAST) calculates the accuracy and consistency of the spacing of aircraft on final approach so that the ATC workload, particularly that of the final director, is reduced. The system determines the most efficient times and positions for aircraft turning onto base leg and final approach.

OSYRIS Arrival Manager

A further development at the five London airports involves a special planning tool known as the Arrival Manager, which calculates the arrival sequence of aircraft approaching London. The sequence is established much earlier than previously, optimising the traffic flows and resulting in fuel savings and reduced emissions. The time taken by aircraft at the various holding points around London will be cut by around 50 per cent.

It is estimated that around 300,000 tonnes of CO_2 will be saved annually, equal to the fuel used by 2,000 jumbo jets. In the morning rush hour, the equivalent of the fuel used by 100 747s would be saved in a year.

The Arrival Manager was introduced at Heathrow and Gatwick in 2009.

London Heathrow

London Heathrow is a busy and complex airport, handling more international traffic than any other airport in the world. In normal operating conditions one runway is used for departures while the parallel runway handles arrivals. Under a local agreement runway 'switching' takes place every day at around 07.00hrs and 15.00hrs UTC, giving the residents under the flight paths some relief from the almost continuous streams of daytime traffic. However, no night-time flights are normally permitted.

There is now pressure in some quarters for mixed-mode operations, under which each runway is used both for arrivals and departures. This would provide an important improvement in the volume of traffic that could be handled.

Arrivals are under the jurisdiction of London Terminal Control, based at Swanwick, as they enter the airspace around London and southeast England. Controllers direct the aircraft to one of the four holding points, then as they leave the stack they are handed over to Heathrow's controllers in the airport tower.

The control tower at Heathrow contains the visual control room (VCR), the glazed room at the top. The VCR team consists of the Ground Movement Planner, the Ground Movement Controller and their assistants. In the centre of the room the Air Arrivals Controller (AAC) and the Air Departures Controller (ADC) sit alongside each other, facing the two runways in use – the holding point of the departure runway and the touchdown point of the arrival runway. If the runways in use are reversed, the AAC and the

ADC turn to face the opposite direction, facing again the appropriate runways.

Heathrow Departures

Several Standard Instrument Departure routes exist at Heathrow, providing departing aircraft with tracks to follow in various directions, depending on individual destinations. Using SIDs reduces radio air time and allows a detailed route to be given to the pilot in the minimum time.

A number of airports, including Heathrow, are also equipped to pass the clearances via datalink to suitably equipped aircraft, reducing air time even more and minimising the chance of errors in copying down details.

On first contact with the Ground Movement Planner (GMP), the pilot will give his callsign, the stand at which the aircraft is parked, and the weather message identifier. The clearance from ATC will specify the SID and also the secondary radar identity squawk code.

Later, when ready, the pilot will request clearance to start engines from the GMP. When this has been approved, he will then

The new Control Tower at London NATS

be handed on to the Ground Movement Controller who will issue a clearance to push back from the aircraft stand, together with taxying information to the holding point of the departure runway.

An example of the first contact could be:

'Delivery, Speedbird one nine nine, triple seven, stand four one two, information Alpha, QNH one zero one four, clearance for Mumbai please.

Speedbird one nine nine, cleared to Mumbai, Dover four golf departure, squawk zero five five one.

Dover four golf, zero five five one, fully ready, Speedbird one nine nine.

Speedbird one nine nine roger, start approved, hold position, contact Ground one two one decimal seven.

One two one seven, wilco, Speedbird one nine nine.'

Where the clearance has been received by datalink (usually referred to as a PDC – Pre-Departure Clearance) the messages are much shorter:

'Delivery, Speedbird one six three on stand four two zero, information Charlie, QNH one zero one four, with a PDC, request start.

Speedbird one six three, start approved, hold position, contact Ground one two one decimal seven.'

As the aircraft approaches the holding point, the pilot will be asked to monitor the frequency of the Air Departures Controller who will give clearance to enter the active runway, line up and eventually take off.

Shortly after the aircraft is airborne, it will be handed over to a departure radar controller at London Terminal Control for onward clearance along the SID route. On first contact, the message will include the SID identifier, current level (or passing level) and cleared level. The controller will confirm that these details comply with the initial clearance.

Heathrow Arrivals

Arriving aircraft are normally directed to one of the four holding points surrounding Heathrow, following a STAR or Standard Arrival Route. Each route has an identifier name, a number and a letter code. If it becomes necessary to revise part of the route, the letter code is changed.

The holding points for Heathrow are at Bovingdon and Lambourne to the north, and Ockham and Biggin to the south. The highest flight level at each is FL110, the lowest FL70. Depending on traffic levels, aircraft can be directed to enter the hold at an intermediate level, flying a racetrack pattern and descending at 1,000ft intervals.

Two controllers deal with traffic at each holding point, one bringing the flights into the pattern and laddering them down through the levels. The second controller then takes the flights from the bottom of the stack and directs them towards the final approach.

During quiet periods, the two southerly holds may be handled by one team of controllers. The same will apply to the northerly holds.

After leaving the stacks, the No. 1 Radar Directors bring the two streams of traffic from the south and the north into two flows towards the extended centreline of the runway. When the aircraft are on the base leg, control is passed to the No. 2 Director who combines the two separate flows into one stream of traffic ready for landing. At around six nautical miles from touchdown, control is passed to the Air Arrivals Controller who gives the clearance to land.

After landing, as the aircraft clears the runway, the flight is handed over to the Ground Movement Controller, who directs it via the taxiways to its parking stand.

Occasionally, in quiet periods, or in an emergency, a flight may be cleared on a straight-in approach without being routed via one of the holding points.

Continuous Descent Approaches (CDAs) are being introduced gradually across Europe. A CDA approach means that the aircraft gradually descends towards the glide slope, instead of the traditional approach where the aircraft is descended to FL70 which then has to be maintained for a considerable distance.

CDAs mean less noise for those living under the approach paths, a reduction in emissions and significant fuel savings.

5. Radio Telephony

Voice messaging between pilots and Air Traffic Control is the primary means of communication in aviation and will remain so for many years. Although in some situations it is possible to convey instructions by other means – datalink, for example – no system has yet been devised which is able to cover the variety of situations that can arise and which need human intervention to resolve.

The language of Air Traffic Control has been developed and refined over many years, resulting in a mixture of words and phrases which have very specific meanings, and it is vitally important that pilots clearly understand what is expected of them, especially in unusual and emergency situations. In today's world of long-distance flights, it is quite possible that the aircraft may be flown by two pilots of different nationalities talking to numerous air traffic controllers whose first language is not English, creating situations where misunderstandings can arise.

English is used throughout the world for international Air Traffic Control messages, but those whose first language is not English can often fail to comprehend instructions. Investigations into incidents and accidents have shown that poor language has often been a factor in the chain of events leading up to an incident. It is essential that aircrew and controllers, especially those who do not use English as their first language, adopt and follow agreed procedures to ensure that phrases and words are clearly understood.

At an international level, the International Civil Aviation Organization has implemented a process of ensuring that pilots and controllers attain a certain standard of English comprehension, not just for aviation language but for non-routine events and emergencies where the ability to communicate clearly is vital.

Surprisingly, in spite of this evidence, many pilots (including English-speaking ones) often fail to follow some of the basic rules, or use sloppy and casual language, which can have the potential for confusion. Controllers in the US are often criticised for using slang and unconventional language which may confuse non-English-speaking pilots. Controllers in the UK, on the other hand, have a reputation for their professional and responsible approach.

In countries where English is not the first language, the national tongue is normally used for internal flights, even though the aircraft may be under the control of a centre dealing with international flights. For example, the pilot of an Air France flight between Paris and Nice will almost certainly use French throughout the trip.

Aeronautical Radio Transmitter
Author

In 2000, at Charles de Gaulle Airport, Paris, an MD83 taking off from the runway collided with a Shorts 330, with fatal consequences. Part of the investigation revealed that the use of French to one aircraft and English to the other meant that the crew of the Shorts 330 did not realise that the MD83 had been cleared for take-off. After this accident, Air France announced that its pilots were to use English at all times, but this proposal had to be hastily withdrawn when strike action was threatened.

Communication Systems

Two systems are in use for communications between aircraft in flight and ground-based control centres, and the worldwide exchange of messages between ground facilities.

The first is the Aeronautical Mobile Service (AMS), which covers communications between the ground and aircraft, dealing with all messages necessary to ensure the safety of flights. The full system title for VHF and UHF radio is Amplitude Modulated Double Side Band (AM-DSB).

Second, the Air Traffic Services Messaging Management Centre (AMC), operated by EUROCONTROL, integrates the Aeronautical Fixed Telecommunications Network (AFTN), the Common ICAO Data Interchange Network (CIDIN) and the ATS Message Handling System (AMHS) to deliver operational ATS Messages such as flight plans between users, Air Navigation Service Providers and airlines, et cetera on a global basis.

The AFTN system is a network joining all units concerned with aviation (airports, airlines, control centres, weather centres and the like), each with a unique eight-bit coded address, which permits a message generated anywhere within the system to be routed worldwide.

ATC Phraseology

The International Civil Aviation Organization (ICAO), based in Montreal, Canada, with a European office in Paris, is responsible for radiotelephony (RT) phraseology procedures which are generally followed by all aviation authorities, although individual States may decide to publish variations (known as 'differences') to some of the procedures to match local circumstances. These procedures are described and illustrated in documents issued by the ICAO and the relevant State aviation authorities.

The main international publication for RT phraseology is the ICAO document PANS-RAC Doc 4444 RAC 501 (*Procedures for Air Navigation Services – Rules of the Air and Air Traffic Services*), which is part of the publication *Procedures for Air Navigation Services – Air Traffic Control*, originally prepared by the Air Traffic Control Committee of the International Conference on North Atlantic Route Service Organisation in Dublin in 1946.

Another important document is the ICAO Manual of Radiotelephony (Document 9432 – AN/925), revised in 2007, which contains many examples of phraseology in common use in Air Traffic Control. It is a lengthy publication which covers numerous situations encountered in ATC; the examples are shown clearly by a system of illustrated diagrams. In the foreword the importance of correct, concise and unambiguous messages is stressed, together with the fact that the person issuing or receiving a message may not use English as a first language. In such cases, messages should be spoken slowly, clearly and without the use of slang or colloquial words.

There are two publications which cover radiotelephony procedures in the UK. The primary source of information is the detailed *Manual of Air Traffic Services (CAP 493)*, together with a handbook entitled the *Radiotelephony Manual (CAP 413)*. Both these documents, including any revisions, can be accessed free of charge on the internet through the Civil Aviation Authority website.

Throughout this book the examples follow the procedures quoted in CAP 413 unless stated otherwise.

The Phonetic Alphabet

In order to standardise the use of the English language, the alphabet is represented phonetically in accordance with the following list. Whenever clarification is required words are spelled out using this alphabet.

Letter	Word	Pronunciation
A	Alpha	AL FAH
B	Bravo	BRAH VOH
C	Charlie	CHAR LEE
D	Delta	DELL TAH
E	Echo	ECK OH
F	Foxtrot	FOKS TROT
G	Golf	GOLF
H	Hotel	HOH TELL
I	India	IN DEE AH
J	Juliet	JEW LEE ETT
K	Kilo	KEY LOH
L	Lima	LEE MAH
M	Mike	MIKE
N	November	NO VEM BER
O	Oscar	OSS CAH
P	Papa	PAH PAH
Q	Quebec	KEH BECK
R	Romeo	ROW ME OH
S	Sierra	SEE AIR RAH
T	Tango	TANG GO
U	Uniform	YOU NEE FORM
V	Victor	VIK TAH
W	Whiskey	WISS KEY
X	X-ray	ECKS RAY
Y	Yankee	YANG KEY
Z	Zulu	ZOO LOO

Numerals are pronounced in accordance with the following table:

0 ZE-RO
1 WUN
2 TOO
3 TREE
4 FOW-er
5 FIFE
6 SIX
7 SEV-en
8 AIT
9 NIN-er

Numbers involving altitude, height, cloud height, visibility and runway visual range which contain whole hundreds and whole thousands are to be transmitted by pronouncing the number of hundreds or thousands separately, using the words 'Hundred' or 'Tousand' as appropriate. For example:

'Climb to altitude two tousand five hundred feet.'

'The runway visual range for runway two seven left is one tousand five hundred metres.'

The digits are spoken separately when referring to callsigns, altimeter settings, flight levels (except FL100, 200, 300 and 400) headings, windspeeds, wind direction, transponder squawk codes and radio frequencies. For example:

'Continental two four seven, contact London on one two seven decimal four three zero.'

'Ryanair four six nine, squawk two six seven seven.'

References to time are normally given using minutes only, except where there could be some confusion. Again, the digits are spoken separately. For example:

'Midland six five two, your approved departure time is now two three.'

'Lufthansa one six two estimating TALLA at four eight.'

(meaning 23 minutes past the hour and 48 minutes past the hour respectively).

Where decimals are involved, the word is pronounced Day See Mal, for example, 'One Two Five Decimal Eight Five Zero'. However, in practice the word is frequently omitted.

Message Priorities

Messages are classified into types and priorities, as set out below:

- 1st priority – distress messages, identified by the prefix 'Mayday' spoken three times.
- 2nd priority – urgent messages, identified by the prefix 'Pan-Pan' spoken three times.
- 3rd priority – messages concerning direction finding.
- 4th priority – flight safety messages, including ATC messages and position reports.
- 5th priority – messages concerning meteorology.
- 6th priority – flight regularity messages (known as company messages).

Transmissions

Pilots of aircraft under the control of a particular sector team will be able to hear the transmissions from the controller, as well as transmissions from all other aircraft in the area using the same frequency.

Before attempting to establish contact with a controller, therefore, the pilot must listen on the particular frequency to check that no other transmissions are taking place. Once this is reasonably certain the pilot will attempt to contact the controller. Most pilots include relevant information about their flight as part of their first transmission on each new frequency, without waiting to check if the controller is actually receiving the message. For example:

'London, good morning Speedbird one one seven passing flight level one two zero cleared flight level one five zero, heading two eight five.'

In the event of a failure to make contact, the pilot will return to the last frequency on which successful transmissions were made and explain that no contact can be established. The controller will then check with the next sector and possibly give the pilot an alternative radio frequency.

The readability (i.e. the clarity of transmissions) is expressed in accordance with the following scale:
- Readability 1 – Unreadable
- Readability 2 – Readable now and then
- Readability 3 – Readable but with difficulty
- Readability 4 – Readable
- Readability 5 – Perfectly readable.

Communication Services

There are three kinds of aeronautical communication service:
- Air Traffic Control, using licensed ATC officers, who are regulated by the Civil Aviation Authority.
- Flight Information Service, which can only be provided by licensed aerodrome flight information service officers (AFISOs), who are regulated by the Civil Aviation Authority; the callsign used is *Information*.
- Air/Ground Communications at aerodromes, provided by unlicensed radio operators who have a certificate of competency for radio operations from the Civil Aviation Authority. The callsign used is *Radio*.

AFISOs at aerodromes may pass instructions to aircraft and other vehicles on the ground, but information only to aircraft in flight. For example, to indicate that there is nothing to prevent an aircraft taking off, the phrase *'take off at your discretion'* will be used.

Air/Ground operators, however, are not permitted to use the expression *'at your discretion'*.

Information passed to an aircraft is to be acknowledged by the use of the callsign or the word *'Roger'* and the callsign. Phrases such as *'Roger, copy the traffic'* should not be used.

Pilots shall notify AFISOs or Radio Operators before changing frequency. Where a flight is under some degree of control, changes of frequency will be given by the controller.

Clearances and other messages are to be spoken reasonably slowly since they may have to be written down by one of the crew.

Where a clearance originates from another unit, this will be stated in the message. For example, a departing flight from an airport, planning to enter controlled airspace, will be given a clearance starting with the words *'London Control clears Air France three three seven to ....'*

Messages transmitted from aircraft should refer at the start of the broadcast to the designation of the service being called. This could be an airport approach control unit, or one of the UK control centres, London or Scottish. Messages for these centres are prefixed **London Control** and **Scottish Control** respectively. In practice it is usual for the full title to be used only on first contact, after which they are commonly referred to as **London and Scottish**, or they may even be omitted altogether. In Irish airspace the equivalent centre is at Shannon with the callsign **Shannon Control**.

Aerodrome control messages are prefixed with the name of the aerodrome and the type of service. For example, *Heathrow Approach, Manchester Ground, Gatwick Delivery* and so on.

Information service messages are preceded by the name of the service, for example *London Information, Scottish Information*.

Air Traffic Service Units (ATSUs) are identified by the following suffixes:

Aerodrome Control	*Tower*
Ground Movement Control	*Ground*
Ground Movement Planning	*Delivery*
Approach Control	*Approach*
Radar (in general)	*Radar*
Approach Radar Control	*Arrival/Dep*
	(*Radar* when combined)
Precision Approach Radar Control	*Talk down*
Area Control (e.g. London)	*Control*
Flight Information	*Information*
Air/Ground Radio	*Radio*

Aircraft Callsigns

The majority of civil transport aircraft use callsigns which have been allocated by the airline concerned, together with a flight

Etihad Airways A330 –243 Shaun Grist

number. In many cases the first part of the callsign will be the actual name of the airline.

British Airways, however, is an exception, using the callsign *Speedbird* for all its flights, apart from the internal Shuttle flights, which use *Shuttle*.

Following the first part of the callsign there will usually be a three - or four-character number or combination of numbers and letters. Many callsigns have been in use for a considerable time, some for more than 20 years.

Many airlines, including BA, use callsign numbers which do not match the actual flight number quoted in timetables. For example, BA flights between London Heathrow and Jersey use 16 for all outbound flights and 17 for all inbound flights, followed by a letter. Between Heathrow and Newcastle flights use 12 outbound and 13 inbound. It is therefore difficult to determine which route an aircraft is on without access to this information.

Other types of callsigns are mainly numerical, for example N456789. After using the full callsign on making first contact, the flight may then use an abbreviated callsign with the last three digits, for example *November 789*.

Aircraft without flight numbers are referred to by the aircraft registration, which is quoted in full on first contact. For example, G-ABCD, on initial contact would be *Golf Alpha Bravo Charlie Delta*. After contact has been established, and provided there is no risk of confusion with other aircraft, the callsign may be abbreviated to *Golf Charlie Delta*.

Several airlines use callsigns which combine numbers with a letter code. The numerical element may relate to part or all of the timetable number, while the letters are applied as a kind of code which may or may not bear a resemblance to the airports concerned. Some airlines use the same callsign number for outbound and inbound flights, adding the letter 'A' for those leaving the UK and the letter 'B' for returning flights.

Callsign Confusion

Confusion between flights with similar callsigns continues to be a problem in busy airspace. Studies over the last few years have shown that several factors have the potential to cause mistakes and if these were addressed by operators the problem would be significantly reduced.

For example, two-thirds of flights use only numbers in the callsign but account for four out of five reports of confusion. The evidence is that a combination of letters and numbers reduces the chance of error considerably. However, operators still need to be careful when deciding on callsigns so that other misinterpretations do not arise.

The following examples give some indication of the chances of two callsigns being misunderstood:

- The use of 4 numbers which are in a different order, e.g. BAW5746 and BAW5476.
- The use of three- and four-digit callsigns, e.g. BAW4566 and BAW566.
- The use of suffixes which can confuse controllers, e.g. letters LL which might be interpreted as the aircraft destination of Heathrow.
- The use of numbers which can be confused with flight levels, e.g. BAW370.

- Combinations of numbers and letters which are difficult to say.

Finally, as an extra safety net, operators should arrange their schedules so that there is a minimum of two hours between the departure times of flights with similar callsigns, so that they are unlikely to be in the same airspace at the same time.

Controllers must always be vigilant when there are similar callsigns on a frequency, warning pilots and carefully checking readbacks, especially when the pilots are not English speaking.

Eventually, when messages are exchanged between control units and aircraft by datalink, the use of unique aircraft identifiers will eliminate the possibility of messages being acted upon by a flight for which it was not intended. Until this day comes, vigilance and care on the part of controllers and pilots are essential, together with careful consideration of callsigns which are easy to confuse.

Message Formats

The initial call made by en route traffic entering UK airspace will establish contact with ATC on the radio frequency given by the previous sector. The same procedure applies when a flight has just departed from an airport. The transfer of control from one air traffic unit to the next will have been co-ordinated usually by telephone, computer link or standing agreement between the controllers involved, so that the new controller will be fully aware of the flight prior to the transfer taking place.

The first call should be in the following form:
A. Full callsign of the addressee
B. Full callsign of the originator
C. The text of the message.

For example:
A. *'London Control*
B. *American three seven*
C. *Flight level one four zero routeing direct to Southampton.'*

The 'London' controller at Swanwick will respond by acknowledging the first call and will continue by giving the flight its clearance:

A. *'American three seven*
B. **London Control**
C. **Climb flight level three two zero, route from your present position direct to Lands End.'**

Brief courtesies such as 'Good morning' are often included, although they are not part of the official phraseology. More examples are given later.

Readbacks

Certain information given by ATC must be read back by the pilot to ensure correct receipt and understanding. The messages requiring readback are given in the UK Aeronautical Information Publication; details are listed below:

- Level instructions
- Heading instructions
- Speed instructions
- Airways or route clearances
- Runway-in-use
- Clearance to enter, land on, take off, backtrack, cross or hold short of an active runway
- Squawk codes
- Altimeter settings
- VDF information
- Frequency changes
- Type of service

Controllers are to prompt a pilot if a readback is not immediately forthcoming. Errors in a readback must be corrected by the controller, and the pilot must then read back the corrected version.

However, in spite of careful attention to detail in RT procedures, errors and misunderstandings do sometimes occur. The human mind can play tricks with speech, and pilots and controllers occasionally say words or phrases which are not intended, even though they are convinced that they have acted correctly. It is only when audio tapes are played back that the error can be revealed. In many cases, a failure to listen carefully can result in

messages being taken by the wrong aircraft, especially where similar callsigns are involved. Non-English-speaking pilots may also mishear or misunderstand instructions; therefore controllers need to take this into account.

Instructions that contain numbers, especially when these involve more than one instruction in the same message, are at particular risk. Simple confusion can occur when, for example, a heading is misheard as a flight level, for example three two zero degrees is interpreted as flight level three two zero, especially if the pilot is anticipating a clearance to that level.

Controllers should not issue more than two instructions in the same transmission. Where additional messages are required, the controller should wait for the correct readback of the first instruction.

For example, there is a risk of mistakes occurring if the following message were transmitted, especially if the pilot changed frequency before the controller checked the readback:

'Virgin twelve, turn right heading two eight zero degrees, climb flight level two six zero and contact London on one three two decimal zero.'

This contains a lot of information for the pilot to absorb and translate into action, especially during a high workload.

Following first contact and the exchange of the necessary messages, two-way communication may continue without the need to wait for an acknowledgment of each call, although routine messages are usually very brief. The ground station callsign may also be omitted.

As the aircraft approaches the limit of a particular sector, the controller will instruct the flight to change radio frequency to the next ATS unit, including its name. For example:

'Speedbird six four four, contact Brest Control on one three three decimal four two five.'
'Iberia nine two seven report your heading to Manchester Approach on one one eight decimal five seven five.'

Understanding ATC Transmissions

ATC messages are constructed from a mixture of standard words and phrases, many of them with very specific meanings, and they follow a logical and carefully organised structure. This is designed to ensure consistency and reliability so that possible misunderstandings are eliminated as far as possible. Sometimes messages may appear to be casual, but in fact they do follow a formal routine in most cases, although situations do arise where plain language is appropriate.

Certain basic rules govern ATC phraseology, as follows:

Measurement Systems

An unusual combination of measurements is used in European ATC, some imperial and some metric, which can be seen by comparing the following:

- Distances used in navigation, position reports, and so on, generally in excess of two or three nm – Nautical miles and tenths, but spoken as 'miles'
- Distance from cloud – Metres
- Relatively short distances such as those relating to aerodromes (eg runway

US Airways A330 – 323X Shaun Grist

lengths, distances of obstructions from the runway or of facilities from the aerodrome where accuracy of greater than one-tenth of a nautical mile is required) – Metres
- Radar-position reporting and distance from touchdown – Nautical miles and fractions thereof, but spoken as 'miles'
- Radar-azimuth displacement from final approach track – Metres
- Altitudes, elevations and heights – Feet
- Depths of snow and slush – Centimetres or millimetres
- Horizontal speed including wind speed – Knots
- Vertical speed – Feet per minute
- Wind direction for landing and taking off – Degrees magnetic
- Wind direction except for landing and taking off – Degrees true
- Visibility – Kilometres and metres
- Runway Visual Range – Metres
- Altimeter setting – Millibars
- Temperature – Degrees Celsius
- Weight – Metric tonnes or kilograms
- Time – Hours and minutes, the day of 24 hours beginning at midnight UTC.

In other parts of the world, different units of measurement may be used. For example, flight levels can be measured in metres and barometric pressure may be quoted in inches of mercury.

The measurements in use are essentially metric, although it has been recognised that certain units outside the Système International d'Unités (SI) system have a special place in aviation and for that reason have been retained for an indefinite period of time. In the UK, the principal measurements treated as exceptions are the nautical mile, the knot, and the foot when used in relation to levels. There are a number of other differences from the ICAO standards, which are set out in the UK Aeronautical Information Publication.

Distances

Distances used in aviation, and shown on radio navigation charts, are referred to in nautical miles. One nautical mile is equal to 6,080ft compared with 5,280ft to a statute mile. The following may be used to convert nautical miles into statute miles or kilometres:

- Multiply nautical miles by 1.85 to obtain kilometres
- Multiply nautical miles by 1.15 to obtain statute miles
- Multiply statute miles by 1.6 to obtain kilometres
- Multiply statute miles by 0.87 to obtain nautical miles
- Multiply kilometres by 0.54 to obtain nautical miles
- Multiply kilometres by 0.62 to obtain statute miles

Distance Measuring Equipment (DME) carried on board aircraft receives radio transmissions from ground beacons and enables the distance to or from that particular point to be displayed to the pilot automatically, enabling the Flight Management System to be programmed as required. For example:

'KLM six six five descend when ready flight level two two zero to be level two zero DME before Clacton.'

Aircraft Speeds

The speed of aircraft is measured in knots (nautical miles per hour) at lower levels, and by Mach numbers at higher levels. This means that speed is quoted as a ratio of the speed of sound, named after the Austrian physicist Ernst Mach (1838–1916). Most passenger jet aircraft cruise at speeds around Mach 0.8. Cruising speeds are important in flight planning for controllers, and the Mach number technique provides a reliable and effective means of ensuring separation.

However, the speed of sound is not constant but decreases with a reduction in temperature which occurs with an increase in altitude. For example, it is 660 knots at mean sea level and 589 knots at FL300.

Various other terms are used in aviation to differentiate between speeds. These are:

- True airspeed
- Indicated airspeed
- Ground speed
- Mach number

True airspeed (TAS) is the actual airspeed of the aircraft through the air. TAS is shown on aircraft flight plans and controllers' flight progress strips. TAS increases with altitude, due to the thinner atmosphere; therefore the aircraft has to travel faster in order to maintain the same air pressure.

Indicated airspeed (IAS) is the speed indicated by the instruments, and is used by pilots in relation to the aircraft performance and its upper and lower speed limits. IAS operates in the opposite way to TAS due to the lower density of the air at higher altitudes. The airspeed indicators under-read at high levels, meaning that the speed of the aircraft is actually greater than shown.

At sea level, indicated air speed and true air speed are the same, but as altitude increases an aircraft at a constant indicated air speed will show an increasing true air speed. For example, at 43,000ft, an IAS of 250 knots is equal to a TAS of 502 knots. Speed limits imposed by Air Traffic Control at the lower levels are expressed as indicated air speed.

Ground speed is the true airspeed of the aircraft over the surface after the effect of wind has been taken into account. For example, an aircraft flying at 300 knots TAS into a headwind of 50 knots will have a ground speed of 250 knots.

Mach number is true airspeed expressed as a decimal of the speed of sound. (The speed of sound varies according to temperature and air density – a colder temperature and a lower air density resulting in a slower speed.) At sea level, for example, Mach 1 (the speed of sound) is 661 knots TAS, whereas at 36,000ft Mach 1 is 572 knots TAS. This remains constant up to around 70,000ft. An aircraft which is climbing to FL350 at a Mach number of 0.7 will gradually reduce speed from 463 knots to 400 knots. Conversely, if an aircraft is descending at a constant Mach number its speed will increase.

Aircraft speeds are expressed in terms of Mach numbers at high levels and indicated air speeds at lower levels, usually changing from one to the other at around FL290. This is because Mach number speed increases as the aircraft descends, and indicated air speed is more accurate at lower levels.

An aircraft descending at Mach .76 will continue until the indicated air speed reaches 290 knots, usually at around FL290. During the descent, the aircraft will be speeding up slightly. The pilot will now switch to IAS and descend at a constant 290 knots. The TAS will decrease from 445 knots to 334 knots. At FL100 the pilot will usually reduce speed to around 210 knots IAS.

Controllers have to understand the relationship between the speed controls and their effect on aircraft performance. Pilots normally expect to descend at a set speed and rate of descent; therefore controllers must plan speed restrictions in advance. For example, a high descent rate and a low airspeed will not be acceptable. In addition, asking a pilot to speed up in one sector, only to slow down in the next, must be avoided.

Levels

Three terms are used in air traffic control to describe the vertical distance of an aircraft

above the surface of the earth:
- flight levels
- altitude
- height.

Flight Levels

Aircraft above the transition level in UK airspace (usually 3,000ft or 6,000ft) will fly at flight levels, reported as two- or three-digit numbers, being the level in thousands of feet with the last two digits omitted. In some parts of the world metres are used instead of feet.

For example, flight level three seven zero indicates a flight level of approximately 37,000ft; flight level two four zero is approximately 24,000ft; flight level nine zero is approximately 9,000ft and so on.

The correct phraseology is *'Flight level three seven zero'* except that in UK airspace flight levels 100, 200, 300 and 400 are spoken as *'hundreds'*. For example, *'Flight level three hundred'*. This variation was originally introduced for FL100, to avoid confusion with FL110.

Altitude

The term 'altitude' is used to indicate the vertical position of an aircraft above mean sea level, using the local area barometric pressure setting, identified by the letters 'QNH'.

Height

The term 'height' is used to indicate the vertical position of an aircraft above the surface of the earth (in virtually all cases this will be the actual runway surface) using the local airfield barometric pressure setting, identified by the letters 'QFE'.

An understanding of these terms, and their relationship to each other, is vitally important for the safety of flight and needs to be explained in more detail.

The Effect of Pressure Variations

The instrument on board an aircraft used to measure its distance above the earth is called the altimeter, a device which reacts to atmospheric pressure. Atmospheric pressure is greatest at sea level, but as the distance above the earth increases so atmospheric pressure decreases, and this drop in pressure can be measured on a scale on the altimeter, calibrated to indicate hundreds and thousands of feet.

However, atmospheric pressure changes almost constantly, as anyone listening to the daily weather forecast will know. 'Low pressure' and 'high pressure' are familiar terms, and as the atmospheric pressure changes so the altimeter reading varies. This means that for the altimeter to give a correct reading it has to be set to the current pressure.

In addition, as the aircraft flies from one area to the next the altimeter pressure setting has to be corrected otherwise it will give a false reading. If an aircraft is being flown using a pressure setting which is lower than the actual pressure, the aircraft will actually be lower than the level indicated by the instruments, and the reverse is also true.

For high-level long-distance flights, having to readjust the altimeter throughout the journey is clearly impractical, so a system has been devised enabling aircraft to operate safely regardless of the variations in atmospheric pressure. This method uses Standard Pressure Settings.

Standard Pressure Settings

The international system uses a theoretical atmospheric pressure, known as the Standard Pressure Setting (or SPS) of 1013.25 millibars (or 29.92 inches) regardless of the actual atmospheric pressure. All aircraft flying above transition level will have their altimeters set to this standard setting. Therefore, all aircraft at FL370, for example, will be at the same level even though it may not actually be 37,000ft. They will only be at 37,000ft if the atmospheric pressure happens to be 1013.25 millibars.

Whether or not the true pressure is 1013.25 millibars is irrelevant, because as all aircraft are on the same setting any variation in the actual level will be common to all.

In many other countries, principally the US, pilots do not use millibars but instead

Finnair Embraer ERJ – 190 Shaun Grist

use inches of mercury. Great care has to be taken by international flight crews who may sometimes confuse the two systems.

QFE and QNH

Below transition altitude, vertical distances are described by two distinct terms, both of which rely on actual barometric pressures for the area in which the aircraft is operating. Air traffic controllers will provide pilots with two separate barometric pressure settings, known by the abbreviations QFE and QNH. (Pilots sometimes refer to these as *'Fox Echo'* and *'November Hotel'* respectively.)

QFE is the local atmospheric pressure setting, which when set on the aircraft's altimeter will cause the instrument to read zero when the aircraft is on the runway. When this setting is in use, the term used to refer to vertical distance is 'height'.

QNH is also the local atmospheric pressure setting, but means that when this is set on the altimeter, the reading on the aircraft instruments will be in feet above mean sea level. This is very important for ensuring that aircraft maintain a safe distance above obstacles on the ground, hills, mountains and so on, which are all shown on charts and maps in feet above mean sea level. It is also vitally important for aircraft in low-level holding patterns where accuracy in remaining vertically separated is paramount. The term used to describe this vertical distance is 'altitude'.

Air pressure falls by one millibar for approximately every 30ft rise in distance above sea level. Therefore, the difference in millibars between the airfield QFE setting and the local area QNH setting multiplied by 30 will give the airfield elevation above mean sea level. For example, if the QFE is given as 997 millibars and the QNH is given as 1012 millibars, the difference (15) multiplied by 30 gives the airfield elevation of approximately 450ft. The difference between QFE and QNH will always be the same for each airport.

The Importance of Pressure Settings

The concept of flight levels, altitude and height, and their safety implications, is often difficult to grasp, so a practical example may be useful.

Flight levels operate at a standard pressure of 1013.25 millibars, regardless of the actual pressure at the time. The base of the imaginary column of air (Flight Level Zero) will only coincide with the mean sea level if the actual pressure is the same (i.e. 1013.25 millibars).

Imagine the air pressure on a particular day to be 978 millibars; this is 35 millibars lower than the standard 1013.25 millibars. Since each millibar is equivalent to a change of approximately 30ft the resulting difference between the actual pressure and the standard pressure is 35 times 30, i.e. 1,050ft – say 1,000ft for our purposes.

In this example, the mean sea level pressure is 978 millibars. The theoretical pressure of 1013.25 millibars is therefore approximately 1,000ft lower than the actual sea level. This means that an aircraft flying with a QNH setting of 978 at 7,000ft would be at the same level as an aircraft flying at FL80 on the standard setting, the pressure difference accounting for the discrepancy in levels. The aircraft using the QNH setting would actually be at 7,000ft, but the aircraft on the standard setting would be flying 1,000ft lower than the instruments indicate.

This explains why it is so important to flight safety that aircraft crews take extreme care when approaching the transition level, either climbing or descending, to ensure that the correct pressure setting is used. There have been numerous examples where aircraft in terminal areas have lost separation for this reason.

For example, aircraft en route to Heathrow normally descend to FL70 in the holding stacks, while departing flights are restricted to a maximum altitude of 6,000ft. When the barometric pressure is low, as in our example earlier, the lowest flight level for arriving aircraft is raised to FL80 so that the risk of losing separation is eliminated.

In the USA the transition level is 18,000ft – much higher than in the UK. American pilots flying in European airspace often refer to levels below 18,000ft in altitudes instead of the correct terminology of flight levels. Controllers have to be careful to ensure that the pilot corrects the readback in view of the possible confusion and risk if the incorrect pressure setting is used. For example, it is not unusual for American pilots to report *'Climbing to one three thousand'* when in fact they mean *'Climbing to flight level one three zero'*.

Altimeter Setting Regions

For low-flying aircraft operating below the transition level it is clearly essential that they always maintain a safe distance above the surface of the earth and any obstructions. As we have seen, setting an incorrect barometric pressure can result in an aircraft being at a much lower altitude than that shown on the instruments. It is therefore important that pilots are made aware of the local barometric pressure so that they can adjust their altimeters as they proceed with the flight.

To achieve this, the UK is divided into twenty regions, known as ASRs (Altimeter Setting Regions) each with a name, in which a local controller will give the pilot the Regional Pressure Setting or RPS. This is the lowest forecast barometric pressure (expressed as QNH) expected during the next two hours. This means that even in the worst conditions the aircraft will never be lower than the altitude shown on the instruments. Therefore, provided the pilot flies at the minimum safe altitude for a particular area (indicated on local charts), his aircraft will not be in danger of colliding with the ground.

As the flight proceeds across country, the pilot will be given the RPS for the next region. For example:
'Golf Charlie Delta the Portland Regional Pressure setting is nine nine five millibars.'

Another example is:
'All stations – the Chatham Regional Pressure Setting is changing on the hour to nine nine six millibars – new Chatham Regional Pressure Setting nine nine six millibars.'

As the Regional Pressure Setting will be lower than a local airfield QNH, care is needed when approaching the airfield as local traffic will probably be using a different barometric pressure setting.

As an additional precaution, the UK is also divided into four large colour-coded areas (red, covering northern Scotland; blue, covering southern Scotland and the north of England; yellow, covering the Midlands and north Wales; and green, covering south Wales and southern England). These are designed to assist pilots who are unsure of their position. Even if a pilot is lost, he will know roughly where he is, so by referring to a special Terrain Clearance Table, indicating the safe minimum altitudes, he will be able to ensure that the aircraft is always well above the highest ground.

To summarise:
- Flight level describes the vertical distance above the earth when the altimeters are on the standard international pressure setting of 1013.25 millibars.
- Altitude is distance above mean sea level, using the local QNH pressure setting.
- Height is distance above the airfield, using the local QFE pressure setting.

(Note: QNH and QFE are examples of the Q code, which originated when radio messages were transmitted in Morse; a number of terms were simplified by using three-letter codes starting with the letter 'Q'.)

Changes in Level

Several terms are used to denote changes in level. ('Level' is a generic term meaning flight level, altitude or height as appropriate.) It is obviously important that such terms are used correctly, otherwise confusion and misinterpretation could result. However, many pilots still use unofficial terminology in relation to level instructions.

Climb	Instructions involving a change to a higher level include the term *'climb'*.
Descend	Instructions involving a change to a lower level include the term *'descend'*.

	'Descend' means the descent may be commenced at the pilot's discretion, although controllers often add the words *'when ready'*. *'Descend now'* means the descent should be commenced straight away. *'Descend immediately'* means the descent should be commenced immediately, usually due to some kind of urgent situation.
Maintain	An instruction requiring an aircraft to remain at one particular level will include the term *'maintain'*.
Passing	Pilots of aircraft which are descending or climbing use the term *'passing'* to describe the actual level through which the aircraft is passing at the time the message is transmitted. For example: *'Golf Charlie Delta report your passing level.'*
Leaving	Pilots of aircraft which have been cleared to climb (or descend) will notify ATC when they commence the climb (or descent) using the term *'leaving'* (the flight level).
Reaching	Pilots of aircraft arriving at a cleared flight level will report to ATC using the term *'reaching'*.
Approaching	If a flight has been cleared to an intermediate level, after which a further clearance can be expected, the phrase *'approaching'* is used as the flight nears the intermediate level.

Message examples:
'Cactus three five nine climb flight level three three zero.'

'London, Easy four five two passing flight level one two zero, cleared flight level one five zero.
Roger, Easy four five two maintain flight level one five zero on reaching. London Easy four five two reaching and maintaining flight level one five zero.'

'United six golf whiskey descend flight level two eight zero initially, expect further descent to be at flight level one eight zero by MARGO.'

Note: Instructions concerning flight levels do not include the word 'to'. However, instructions concerning altitude or height do include the word 'to' before the words 'altitude' or 'height'.

These examples are correct:
'Climb flight level one five zero.'
'Climb to altitude two thousand five hundred feet.'
'Climb to height one thousand feet.'

These examples are incorrect:
'Climb to flight level one five zero.'
'Climb to two thousand five hundred feet.'
'Climb to one thousand feet.'

The first controller message concerning altitude or height must include the pressure setting. If this is less than 1,000 millibars the word 'millibars' is to be included in the message. This is to avoid situations where the pilot may be used to pressure settings in inches of mercury. For example:
'*Golf Charlie Delta descend to altitude two thousand five hundred feet, QNH nine nine seven millibars*'
(Compare this with two nine seven inches.)

Headings and Tracks

The direction in which an aircraft is flying is known as its heading and is quoted in terms of degrees of the compass, always using three figures, each digit being spoken separately.

If there is no wind to affect the flight, an aircraft flying due east will be on a heading of

090 degrees, due south will be 180 degrees, due west will be 270 degrees and due north will be 360 degrees (often referred to as *'North'*).

Where the wind conditions are a factor, the heading on the aircraft instruments will not be the same as its track over the ground. For example, an aircraft flying on a northerly heading in a westerly wind will actually be tracking to the right. If the controller wants the aircraft to follow a northerly heading he will instruct the pilot to fly on a more westerly heading, possibly 345 degrees.

The term *'continue'* is used by ATC if the aircraft is to remain on the same heading, although the term *'maintain'* is often used incorrectly by pilots in this context.

When a flight is required by ATC to remain on a particular heading it is then said to be on a *'radar heading'*, and this must be continued until advised by ATC. The term *'own navigation'* is used when the flight is not on a radar heading.

Flights may be instructed by ATC to change direction by a specified amount, to continue on a particular heading, or to turn on to a specified heading. Radar headings may only be assigned when flights are under radar control.

The pilot of an aircraft on a radar heading must report the heading when changing radio frequency and speaking to the next controller. Words such as *'steering'* or *'assigned'* in relation to headings are incorrect.

Message examples:
'Lufthansa six six two report heading.
Three two zero degrees Lufthansa six six two.
Roger, Lufthansa six six two continue present heading 'til advised.*
Present heading 'til advised Lufthansa six six two.'

'Air France five eight seven turn left ten degrees and report new heading.
Left ten degrees, new heading will be two eight five degrees Air France five eight seven.
Air France five eight seven, roger, make that a radar heading.
Radar heading two eight five degrees Air France five eight seven.'

'Speedbird one seven seven cancel radar heading, route direct to Cork.'

Privilege Style B757 – 256 Shaun Grist

Note that compass headings are always spoken as three separate figures (*'zero one five degrees'*) whereas instructions to turn are in whole numbers (*'Turn left ten degrees'*) so that possible confusion is avoided.

For example, imagine an aircraft is flying on a heading of 350 degrees. An instruction to turn right *'one five degrees'* would put the aircraft onto a heading of 005 degrees. Alternatively, an instruction to turn onto a heading of *'zero one five degrees'* would require the pilot to turn right 25 degrees.

The Quadrantal Rule

Since aircraft operating outside controlled airspace are not under control, and as an additional safety measure, pilots flying under Instrument Meteorological Conditions above the transition level and below FL195 must fly at flight levels which are in accordance with the Quadrantal Rule, which is intended to ensure that aircraft remain clear of each other by at least 500ft.

Under this rule aircraft flying on magnetic tracks:
- between 000 degrees and 089 degrees, must be flown at odd flight levels
- between 090 degrees and 179 degrees, must be flown at odd flight levels plus 500ft
- between 180 degrees and 269 degrees, must be flown at even flight levels
- between 270 degrees and 359 degrees, must be flown at even flight levels plus 500ft.

Semicircular Cruising Levels

Flight levels in UK-controlled airspace are in accordance with the ICAO system of Semicircular Cruising Levels, under which aircraft on opposite direction tracks are separated by 1,000ft. Aircraft on tracks between 000 and 179 degrees fly at odd flight levels, while those on tracks between 180 and 359 degrees fly at even flight levels.

However, the airspace above (FL290 is designated as Reduced Vertical Separation Minima (RVSM) airspace, and any aircraft

not approved for RVSM flight will be separated from all other traffic by 2,000ft.

The RVSM programme was implemented in April 2001, permitting 1,000ft vertical separation in the London and Scottish FIRs, following its successful introduction in the North Atlantic. Six new flight levels were introduced, creating a substantial increase in airspace capacity. Before the introduction of RVSM, the minimum vertical separation for flights above FL290 was 2,000ft.

In certain circumstances, controllers have discretion to authorise flights to operate at non-standard cruising levels where appropriate, referred to as 'ODLs' (opposite direction levels).

Time

For aviation, the time system is Co-Ordinated Universal Time, a combination of two other methods of time measurement: Universal Time and International Atomic Time. The initials UTC are a compromise agreed by the International Telecommunications Union, which wanted a definition that would be understood throughout the world. Pilots and controllers sometimes shorten it to 'Universal'.

UTC is used internationally as a time standard in aviation, but pilots may also refer to 'local' as the time for the particular time zone they happen to be in.

'Zulu' is also a common term used by some pilots and controllers (mainly the military) to represent time.

In aviation, particularly where long-range journeys are concerned, there is usually no need to refer to hours, and time is normally expressed only in minutes, unless there is likely to be confusion.

Self Positioning

Most modern transport aircraft are provided with sophisticated navigation equipment which enables the pilot to select any position by reference to its latitude and longitude – for example, a reporting point – details of which are stored in the Flight Management System. This enables the aircraft to be automatically flown to any required location, independently of any guidance from ATC or ground-based navigation beacons.

For example, the pilot may request permission to fly the aircraft to a point twenty miles along the extended centreline of the destination airport's landing runway, ready to commence the final approach. This procedure is called self positioning, or centre fix.

Guidance on the use of self positioning procedures has been issued by the Civil Aviation Authority, although it is not an officially recognised ATC procedure. A request to self position will always be at the discretion of ATC, especially where the track could take the aircraft outside controlled airspace.

Message Examples
The examples provide a selection of typical messages where the flight is under radar control. Not included are messages concerning oceanic clearances, airport arrivals and departures, or company messages, as these aspects are covered elsewhere.

POSITION REPORTS
The following items of information may be included in a position report made by the pilot. However, in practice, reports often consist of the callsign and flight level only.

- Aircraft callsign
- Position
- Time
- Level
- Next position
- Estimated time of arrival

'London Control, Air Canada eight seven six approaching Strumble this time, flight level three five zero, estimating Compton at four three.

Air Canada eight seven six, London, good morning, maintain flight level three five zero, route upper lima nine for Frankfurt. Squawk ident on six three zero two.

Roger, maintain flight level three five zero, ident six three zero two, upper lima nine for Frankfurt, Air Canada eight seven six.'

The ATC unit callsign will be included in the message on first contact. Position reports are normally given only on first contact with an ATC unit and not when changing to a different sector.

SPEED CONTROL
'Speedbird one seven six, London, report Mach number.

Mach decimal eight two, Speedbird one seven six.

Roger – break – United three three five, report Mach number.

Decimal eight one, United three three five.

Roger, United three three five, speed not greater than decimal eight one.

Roger, speed not greater than decimal eight one United three three five.

Speedbird one seven six, London, can you increase to decimal eight three for a short while?

Affirm Speedbird one seven six.

Roger, Speedbird one seven six, speed decimal eight three until advised.

Understood, speed decimal eight three until advised Speedbird one seven six.'

CONFLICTING TRAFFIC
'Easy three mike x-ray, maintain flight level three two zero on reaching, opposite direction traffic one thousand above.

Roger, Easy three mike x-ray we'll maintain three two zero on reaching, traffic in sight.'

Pakistan Airlines Boeing 777 Author

'Condor seven three two, increase your rate of climb to flight level two seven zero, crossing traffic at flight level two five zero in your ten o'clock at fifteen miles.'

'Shuttle six mike alpha request climb flight level three two zero.

Shuttle six mike alpha, negative, crossing traffic at that level, I'll give you climb as soon as I can.'

DIRECT ROUTEINGS
'London control, Midland three mike zulu, flight level three five zero, approaching Berry Head, for Glasgow.

Midland three mike zulu London, maintain flight level three five zero, Upper November eight six four for Glasgow, squawk ident on four two six six.

Ident on four two six six, maintain flight level three five zero, Midland three mike zulu. Any direct routeings would be appreciated.

Midland three mike zulu roger, stand by.

Midland three mike zulu, after passing Berry Head you can route direct to Golf Oscar Whiskey.
    After passing Berry Head, direct to the GOW Midland three mike zulu, thanks very much.'

TURBULENCE
'KLM six six one, moderate turbulence at our level, have you had any reports at lower levels?

Stand by – break – Ryanair three eight one, what's the ride like at your level?

It's smooth here Ryanair three eight one.

Thank you – break – KLM six six one, that aircraft is at three two zero, thirty miles ahead of you, reported smooth, do you wish to descend?

Affirm KLM six six one.

Roger, KLM six six one descend flight level three two zero.

Descend flight level three two zero KLM six six one, thank you.'

Other examples of different situations are included in the relevant chapters.

6. The North Atlantic System

The north Atlantic is the world's busiest oceanic airspace, carrying a daily average in excess of 1,000 flights. In spite of the economic downturn in 2008, the volume of oceanic traffic increased slightly compared to the previous year.

For air traffic purposes, the North Atlantic is divided into five main areas: Shanwick, Santa Maria, Iceland, Gander and New York, known as NARTEL – the North Atlantic Radiotelephony Network.

Responsibility for flights operating over the eastern half of the North Atlantic rests with National Air Traffic Services which operates the Oceanic Area Control Centre at Prestwick in Scotland. It will soon move into a new facility, already built on an adjacent site. It is planned to move the military section first, followed by Scottish FIR domestic control, and finally the Oceanic unit.

Oceanic traffic is under the control of this Centre, but messages for most flights are routed through a long-range radio station near Shannon, Ireland. A combination of the two locations – Shannon and Prestwick – resulted in the creation of the callsign Shanwick for the eastern half of the oceanic airspace.

Many commercial flights from across Europe and the American continent pass through UK airspace, generally in two daily flows. Westbound traffic crosses the ocean during the day; eastbound flights during the night and early morning.

Following the terrorist attacks in New York in 2001, there was a significant drop in transatlantic traffic, and it was three years before it was restored to previous levels. The numbers have steadily risen since then,

Controllers at the Oceanic Area Control Centre, Prestwick, dealing with traffic in the Shanwick region of the north Atlantic Author

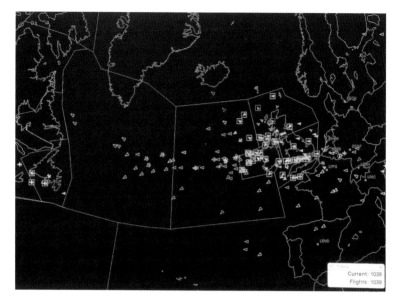

Eastbound North Atlantic Display for ATC planners at Swanwick NATS

although the rate of increase slowed in the latter half of 2008, with continuing reductions during 2009.

MNPS Airspace

Most of the airspace of the North Atlantic between 27,500ft and 42,000ft is Class A and is known as MNPS (Minimum Navigation Performance Specification) airspace. Aircraft are required to satisfy certain criteria concerning their navigation capabilities, as it is important that flights which are out of radar contact must be able to navigate with a very high degree of reliability, especially as traffic in the airspace is beyond any kind of surveillance.

However, the introduction of new technology such as Automatic Dependent Surveillance means that controllers on both sides of the Atlantic now have access to a simulated radar picture of the traffic.

The Organised Track System

Oceanic airspace differs fundamentally from that over the landmasses in that there are no predetermined airways or upper air routes. Instead, a series of routes in each direction are organised so that flights can operate on the most efficient tracks, taking advantage of weather systems which are rarely the same from day to day.

These routes, known as tracks, form the Organised Track System (OTS) and new ones are established twice every 24 hours, once in each direction. As the weather plays a major part in the efficiency of airline operations, the tracks can vary considerably from day to day. For eastbound traffic the high-speed 'jetstreams' can significantly affect the economy of long flights.

Planners at the centres on both sides of the Atlantic, at Gander and Prestwick, consult with each other, and with the airlines, over the daily track allocations, with Gander being responsible for the night-time tracks, and Prestwick for the daytime tracks, including liaison with the other Oceanic Centres in Iceland, New York and Santa Maria.

Eastbound tracks are valid between 01.00 and 08.00 UTC, westbound tracks between 11.30 and 19.00 UTC, the times being

The Operations Room at the new Control Centre at Prestwick before being brought into use
Author

applicable at 30 degrees west. However, the increasing number of very long-range flights means that more aircraft are flying the Atlantic against the traditional flows, and these have to be accommodated by the inclusion of opposite direction tracks.

Once established, the OTS messages giving details of the tracks are passed directly to control centres, airports, the Central Flow Management Unit and the airlines that regularly use the Atlantic. They can also be found on a number of internet sites.

Several tracks are arranged each day, with westbound tracks identified by 'Alpha', 'Bravo', 'Charlie', 'Delta', 'Echo', and so on, 'Alpha' being the

most northerly. Eastbound tracks, from North America to Europe, are defined by letters commencing with 'Zulu' as the most southerly track, followed by 'Yankee' as the next track to the north, then 'X-ray' and so on. Tracks are at least 60 nm apart due to the fact that the aircraft are

An aerial view of the new Control Centre at Prestwick
NATS

Next Generation ATC Suite NATS

beyond radar surveillance. As the technology and reliability improves this will eventually be reduced in stages, providing yet more capacity.

The points at which the tracks join the domestic airspace are known as entry or exit points, although the exit points are often referred to as landfall points.

In the past it was possible to have as many as ten tracks in operation, but with the extra capacity resulting from a reduction in vertical separation from 2,000ft to 1,000ft, five or six are usually sufficient.

Reduced Vertical Separation

After years of research and testing, the various aviation authorities decided that a reduction in the vertical separation between high-level aircraft was feasible, as developments in height-keeping technology improved. The obvious benefit would be a substantial increase in capacity as more flight levels became available. The programme was entitled RVSM or Reduced Vertical Separation Minima.

Consequently, in March 1997, the first stage of the programme was implemented in North Atlantic airspace, permitting suitably equipped aircraft operating between FL330 and FL370 to be vertically separated by 1,000ft instead of 2,000ft as previously. The two new levels, 340 and 360, gave airlines additional options when planning the most efficient flight profiles.

Eventually, after a successful trial period, FL320 and FL380 were introduced, followed by FL300 and FL400 in April 2001, coinciding with the implementation of the RVSM programme in UK and Irish airspace. A year later, RVSM was introduced in mainland Europe, and it is now a worldwide system.

When the programme was in use only over the Atlantic, controllers had to ensure that as flights entered domestic airspace many of them would have to either climb or descend to fit in with the traditional separation standard of 2,000ft, requiring some retraining for controllers.

Height Monitoring

For an aircraft to operate in RVSM it must have the required navigational capability known as MASPS (Minimum Aircraft System Performance Specification). Each State of Registry certifies its aircraft for compliance. To ensure this, a height monitoring unit (HMU) was established near Aberporth, in west Wales, on the centreline of Upper Lima Nine) with a second at Gander in Canada. Special radars track the exact height of each flight as it passes overhead. Similar monitoring radars operate across Europe.

Transition Airspace

Two areas – SOTA, the Shannon Oceanic Transition Area, south of Ireland, and NOTA, the Northern Oceanic Transition Area, to the north – are delegated to controllers at Shannon, enabling them to co-ordinate flights as they approach or leave Shanwick airspace.

Oceanic Clearances

Before a flight is allowed to enter North Atlantic airspace, the crew must obtain an 'oceanic clearance' direct from Shanwick. This is normally done by radio when the aircraft is in flight over the UK, although for those airports close to oceanic airspace their clearances are requested while the aircraft is still on the ground. Two VHF radio frequencies are allocated for oceanic clearances: 123.950 MHz for aircraft registered west of 30 degrees west, and 127.650 MHz for aircraft registered east of 30 degrees west. In practice, this generally means that American and Canadian airlines use 123.950, and British and European airlines use 127.650.

Pilots call Shanwick on one of these frequencies, using the aircraft's second radio, when they are approximately one hour's flying time from the oceanic airspace boundary.

Screen display showing part of the North Atlantic NATS

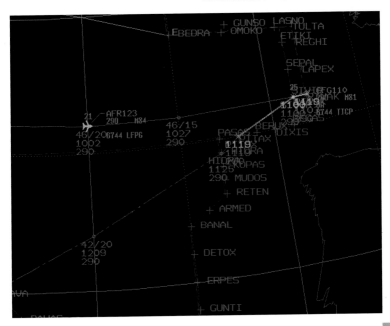

75

The radio stations handling oceanic clearances are at Dundonald Hill (near Prestwick), at Davidstow Moor (Cornwall), Mangersta (Outer Hebrides) and Grantham (Lincolnshire).

An increasing number of aircraft have datalink capabilities, and currently around two-thirds are given clearances using this method.

The message will usually contain the following:

- Callsign **Shanwick**
- Aircraft callsign
- Oceanic entry point
- Estimated time at entry point
- Flight level
- Highest acceptable flight level
- Requested track
- Alternative track
- Requested flight level
- Requested Mach number
- Track message identifier.

Automatic Track Tool at the Oceanic Area Control Centre *Photo courtesy of NATS*

The destination may also be included *'request clearance to Toronto'*,

For example:

'Shanwick, Shanwick, Speedbird one seven seven estimating LIMRI at one five one three, flight level three two zero, maximum three six zero, request clearance to Kennedy on track Delta, alternate Track Echo, flight level three three zero, Mach decimal eight two, TMI one four four.'

At Shanwick, the Clearance Delivery Officer (CDO) inputs the requested flight details into the Flight Data Processing System (FDPS), which is then presented to the appropriate planning controller. The request will be checked against all other flights on the same track, flight level and Mach number and the system carries out a conflict prediction to ensure that the minimum separation will be maintained until the aircraft reaches the other side of the ocean.

For example, one of the preceding aircraft may be at a slower speed, meaning that a following flight may reduce the required

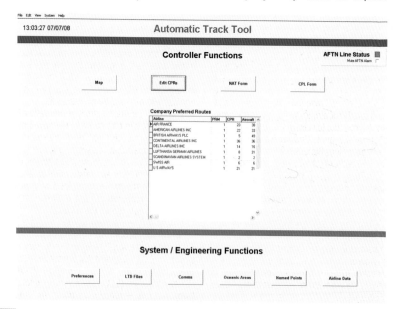

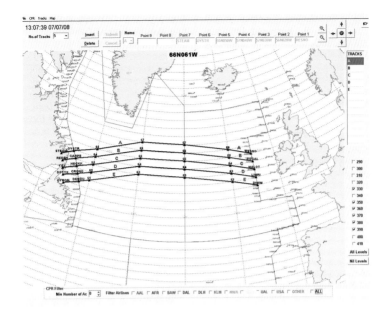

separation to an unacceptable level before it comes under the control of the domestic controllers in Canadian or US airspace. In such cases, the pilot will be offered an alternative level or a slower Mach number, or even a switch to a different track.

Eventually, usually after several minutes, the CDO will call the flight and confirm the clearance or any alternative options until an agreement is reached. In most cases, particularly for airlines which regularly cross the Atlantic, the full clearance will not be read back by the pilot. Once the clearance has been accepted, the pilot will be returned to the domestic ATC frequency.

The daily track message includes a unique reference number based simply on the actual day of the year, known as the Track Message Identification Number (TMI). For example, on the last day of January the TMI will be 031. This confirms to the controller that the pilot is using the correct information.

Approximately one flight every hour will be asked to send meteorological reports as it progresses on its journey, referred to as 'SEND MET'.

North Atlantic Track Examples
Photo courtesy of NATS

Because the weather plays an important part in the flight planning process, it is not uncommon for aircraft to use transatlantic tracks that vary considerably through the year. A flight from Heathrow to New York, for instance, may fly over southwest England on one day and over Northern Ireland the next.

The Mach number technique (the ratio of the aircraft speed compared to the speed of sound at a particular flight level) is used for ensuring separation between successive aircraft in oceanic airspace. Two aircraft at the same flight level and Mach number, and experiencing the same conditions of wind speed and temperature, will maintain the same separation across the Atlantic.

Navigation equipment today is highly accurate, so much so in fact, that two aircraft on the same track will be exactly one above the other. As a safeguard, ICAO introduced a procedure known as the Strategic Lateral Offset Procedure (SLOP), which gives pilots three choices – remain on track; fly one nautical mile right of track; or fly two nautical miles right of track. Flying to the left of track is not permitted. Pilots may opt to use visual means, TCAS or radio communication with other pilots when deciding which option to adopt.

Position Reporting Procedures

Once a flight approaches its cleared oceanic entry point, the pilot will be instructed to continue radio communication with Shanwick using High Frequency radio instead of VHF. This is because VHF radio is dependent on line-of-sight and is of no use in oceanic airspace. For example:

'Speedbird one seven seven, continue with Shanwick on HF, good day.'

The pilot will have two HF radio frequencies to use, known as primary and secondary. This is because HF communications are often noisy and unreliable, so the pilot has the choice of changing from one channel to the other to obtain the best reception.

The messages from aircraft which are using HF radio over the eastern half of the Atlantic are received by radio operators at a relay station at Ballygirreen, near Newmarket-on-Fergus in County Clare, a few miles north of Shannon Airport, operated by the Irish Aviation Authority. Messages are then passed to the Oceanic Area Control Centre at Prestwick. Any responses are returned to Ballygirreen operators who then relay them to the aircraft.

The first message on HF radio will include a request for a 'Selcal' check. This represents 'selective calling' and is a means by which ATC make contact with the flight by transmitting a radio signal containing the Selcal identity. Every aircraft has its own individual

Corsair B747 – 422 Shaun Grist

code, consisting of two pairs of letters. (This is not the same as the squawk code as the Selcal code stays with the aircraft permanently.) In each pair the first letter is earlier in the alphabet than the second. For example, BF-AE is acceptable as a Selcal but not FB-EA.

Selcal means that the crew can discontinue maintaining a listening watch on the aircraft's noisy radio. If the radio operators wish to contact the aircraft, its Selcal is transmitted and this operates a chime signal on the flightdeck.

As the flight progresses across the ocean, the pilots must send position reports at the waypoints on their particular track. These will coincide with whole tens of longitude – for example, 10 degrees west, 20 degrees west, 30 degrees west, 40 degrees west, and so on – and will result in position reports at approximately one-hour intervals.

The report is given in latitude and longitude, except that some points may be given names and in such cases these will be quoted. The next position and an estimate of the time at that position are then given, using the next significant point to be crossed by the aircraft, plus the next position, but without a time estimate. This ensures that the controllers can check that the flight is keeping to its flight plan and is also maintaining separation from other traffic.

Position reports consist of the following:
- the word 'position'
- the aircraft callsign
- present position
- time over (in hours and minutes UTC)
- present flight level
- next position
- time estimate for next position (hours and minutes UTC)
- next position
- additional information – meteorological reports, requests for a change of level or speed, et cetera

The transfer of responsibility from Shanwick to Gander takes place at 30 degrees west; therefore as the aircraft approaches this point the position report will include the words 'copy Gander'. Controllers at Gander will be listening on the same radio frequency. For example:

'Speedbird one one seven, copy Gander, five four north two zero west, one five four two, flight level three eight zero, estimate five four north three zero west one six three nine, next five three north four zero west.'

The majority of flights between Northern Europe and the North American continent will pass through the oceanic regions of Shanwick and Gander – most European flights to Kennedy Airport at New York do not usually enter the New York Oceanic Region.

Shannon Aeradio

The North Atlantic Communications System is operated by the Irish Aviation Authority via the radio station at Ballygirreen. This was established in 1936, making contact with flights in Morse code; this meant that each aircraft had to carry a radio operator to deal with the messages.

The station was originally set up to deal with the flying boats which were based at Foynes in the Shannon estuary, where Pan American flying boat 'Yankee Clipper' completed the first non-stop transatlantic flight in July 1939.

In the same year, the introduction of teletype enabled the rapid handling of flight details, but the big breakthrough came with the development of radiotelephony in 1948 which effectively did away with the need for the additional crew member on board the aircraft.

The station still handles a large volume of traffic, with more than fifty radio operators dealing with over a million messages a year. The development of new technology at Ballygirreen has enabled the station to communicate by High Frequency datalink, a particularly useful method for keeping in touch with flights using the polar routes between the American continent and the Far East, as well as traffic in other areas. Another attraction for the airlines is its relatively low cost in comparison with other systems.

Flight Messages

There are eight classifications of reports made by aircrew:

POS – Position report at each waypoint
across the Atlantic
RCL – Request for a clearance
RBK – Readback (confirmation to the
Oceanic Area Control Centre of the
delivery of an ATC message to a
flight, possibly with a reply from
the flight)
RPE – Report of a revised time estimate
TAM – Technical Acknowledgement
Message
SEL – Selcal
EMG – An emergency message of Urgency
or Distress, for example 'Mayday'
MIS – Miscellaneous messages.

Message Transfer

The transfer of messages between Ballygirreen and Shanwick is by high-speed computer links, using numerous abbreviations to limit the extent of the typescript. All messages commence with the day of the month and the time (for example 161324 indicates the 16th day, time 13.24).

Abbreviations include the following, which are a kind of shorthand used by radio operators at Ballygirreen:

agn – again	lvg – leaving
apsg – after passing	mntn – maintain
bndy – boundary	ms – minus
cfms – confirms	pos – position
clrnce – clearance	req – request
clrsu – clears you	rl – report leaving
est – estimate	rr – report reaching
f – flight level	rrt – reroute
fm – from	tfc – traffic
hier – higher	u – you
lvl – level	una – unable

Aircraft callsigns are given with the three-letter airline codes, for example: BAW176 (Speedbird 176 of British Airways). At the end of the message, the family and the individual frequency is quoted in code – for example TA denotes 'A' family, frequency 5598 kHz.

Reports are made either by voice to the radio operators at Ballygirreen, or by the

Overnight Eastbound Traffic
Photo courtesy of NATS

Controller – Pilot Datalink Communications directly to the Oceanic Centre. Reports received at Ballygirreen are transferred directly to the FDPS computer at Prestwick.

The system automatically checks for errors in the report, bringing them to the attention of the controller for checking and correction. Provided the message is acceptable, the flight data display will be updated. The system will also carry out a conflict probe to ensure that the flight will remain safely separated from other traffic.

Controllers use two adjoining screens to give a visual view in two dimensions of the traffic under their control. One screen shows a simulated picture of the North Atlantic, derived from the flight crew's position report data, displaying details of each flight, including their locations. The second screen lists the aircraft, giving the same information in a textual format.

The list screen shows the flights track by track – eastbound in brown, westbound in blue – with details of the aircraft callsign, departure and destination airports, flight level, Mach number, waypoints, estimated times over each waypoint and aircraft type. Text messages appear on the right-hand side of this screen, alerting controllers to possible conflict problems, overdue position reports, conformance alerts, and so on.

Clicking on a particular flight brings up the complete flight plan,

enabling the controller to decide what action, if any, is necessary. Where a possible loss of separation is anticipated between two flights, the times on the list are highlighted to attract the controller's attention. On the simulated radar screen, the controller can focus on any area of concern or on an individual aircraft as required.

Messages from pilots may be sent by voice, via Ballygirreen, or by controller/pilot datalink communication (CPDLC). These messages appear on the controller's screen as a text message, possibly requesting a change of level or Mach number. The controller's response is typed in the box and is then automatically returned to the sender, either at Ballygirreen or direct to the aircraft. The system is set to inform the controller when the pilot updates the Flight Management System, with an alert if this does not happen within a set period.

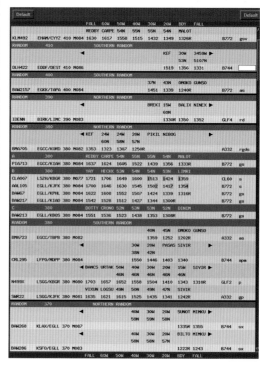

Shanwick Controllers Data
Photos courtesy of NATS

7. Aeronautical Information

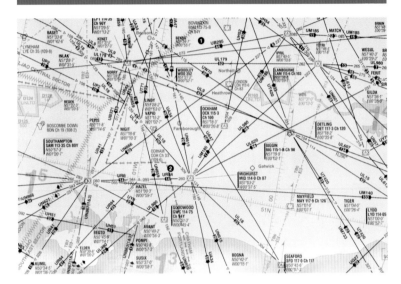

CAUTION – The chart extracts in this publication are shown purely for illustrative purposes. Under no circumstances must the information be relied upon for flight planning, navigation or any other activity related to aviation. Reproductions may not be current and may not be to the original scale.

Introduction
For aviation and airband enthusiasts, charts are an important tool for understanding how airspace is organised and managed. They cover very detailed information on the various air routes and radio facilities worldwide; many are available free of charge via the internet, while others can be purchased at reasonable prices.

There are several suppliers in the UK, as well as EUROCONTROL. They deal with different aspects of the subject, depending on the needs of the user, and cover airways, high-level routes, civilian airports, military airfields and pilots who fly under Visual Flight Rules.

High Level Routes, Southern England
Reproduced by kind permission of the RAF, OC No1 AIDU

Different producers show the same information in different formats and colouring schemes, often covering different parts of the country on individual charts. Each supplier publishes details of its products.

Chart Suppliers
Charts are available from the following organisations:

- Civil Aviation Authority
- EUROCONTROL
- Royal Air Force
- Airplan Flight Equipment Limited
- Navtech European Aeronautical Group
- Jeppesen

Civil Aviation Authority
CAA charts are available from Airplan Flight Equipment, The Pilot Warehouse, Transair

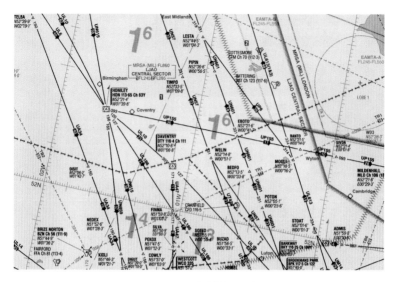

High Level Routes in the Birmingham and Midlands area Reproduced by kind permission of the RAF, OC No1 AIDU

High Level Routes, West Wales Reproduced by kind permission of the RAF, OC No1 AIDU

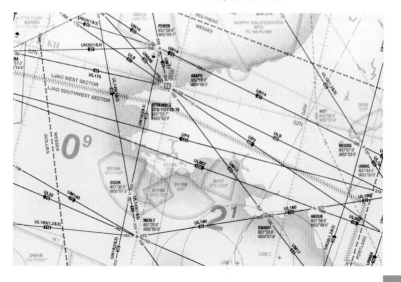

Pilot Shop and Pooleys Flight Equipment. Contact details for each of these organisations can be found in aviation magazines or the internet.

Certain charts, including layouts of all UK airports, Standard Instrument Departure Routes, Standard Arrival Routes, and UK upper and lower airspace may be printed free of charge from the National Air Traffic Services UK Integrated Aeronautical Information Package website – details are given in the Appendix.

Obviously, these charts are limited to the size that can be printed, so charts covering the whole of the UK are too small to be of much use.

The CAA produces large full colour charts for VFR flight covering different parts of the country. These are based on Ordnance Survey maps and are similar in appearance, showing in full colour roads, motorways, towns and other prominent features but with the addition of airways and other areas of controlled airspace.

EUROCONTROL

The Cartography Service of EUROCONTROL produces excellent charts of different parts of European airspace, including one which covers the UK. There are two types: Airspace Management Planning Charts and Central Flow Management Unit (CFMU) charts. The best one for the UK is the CFMU Desk Chart, which is A2 size, reference 03-UK & Ireland, with upper airspace on one side and lower airspace on the reverse. It can be viewed on its website, but not printed.

Charts can be obtained by downloading an order form and catalogue from the website, payment being made by credit card or bank transfer, in Euros. Cheques are not accepted. Once an order has been completed, the customer will receive a new catalogue and price list every year.

Royal Air Force

The RAF No. 1 Aeronautical Information Documents Unit (AIDU), based at Northolt, is responsible for the production and supply of flight information, including charts.

The RAF produces a first-class range of radio navigation charts for the UK and Europe, and for many other parts of the world, on good quality paper. A feature of

High Level Routes, North Wales
Reproduced by kind permission of the RAF, OC No1 AIDU

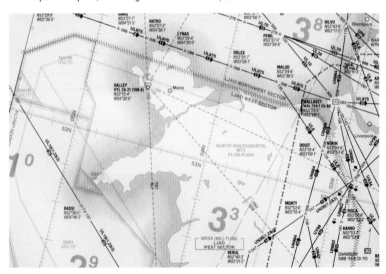

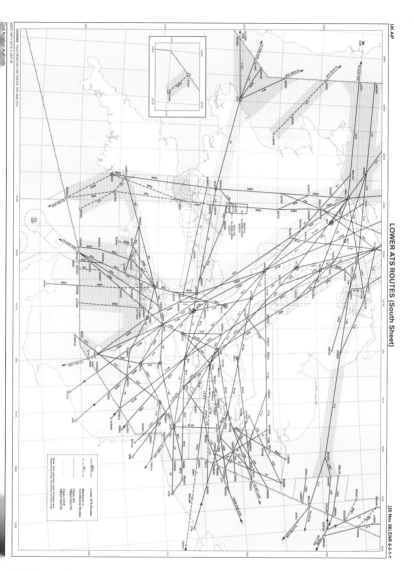

UK Airways System
Reproduced with the permission
of the CAA, copyright CAA

85

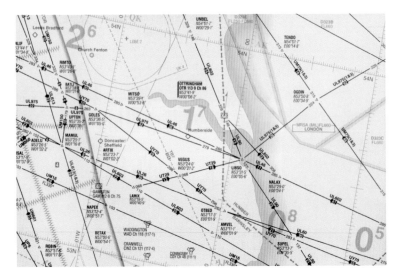

High Level Routes, North East England *(caption, right column)*

these charts is that most military routes, North Sea helicopter routes and other military features are also shown.

Also available to the public are the Flight Information Handbook and the British Isles and North Atlantic En route Supplement. They include very detailed information on aviation procedures and airfields, including military bases.

The catalogue of Flight Information Publications (called FLIPS) is available either by post or via the RAF website. New customers should place an order for the first time by sending payment by cheque with the completed order form. The Customer Services Section will then open an account and future orders may be placed through the website.

Airplan Flight Equipment Limited and Navtech European Aeronautical Group

Both these companies supply Aerad charts, originally part of British Airways, which are probably the most well-known radio navigation charts; they are also available through a number of other sales outlets. The UK charts cover high and low altitude airspace throughout Europe.

They also provide other worldwide charts, including Standard Instrument Departure

High Level Routes, North East England
Reproduced by kind permission of the RAF, OC No1 AIDU

Charts, Standard Arrival Charts, Noise Abatement routes for airports, plans of airports, ramp details and details of docking procedures for various aircraft types. Product details and ordering information can be viewed on their websites.

Jeppesen

Jeppesen charts are available from a number of UK outlets (Transair, for example). They cover a worldwide range of High and Low-Level IFR charts, VFR flight and airfields. However, at the time of writing, and in contrast to the other suppliers, the UK is split across different publications with no one chart covering the whole country.

Many of their radio navigation charts include a comprehensive communications frequency listing on the low-altitude editions. Low-Level VFR charts for the UK are also available.

Understanding the Information

Flights are broadly divided into general aviation – covering mainly light aircraft, often operating outside controlled airspace – and

UPPER AIRSPACE MILITARY TACAN ROUTE SYSTEM

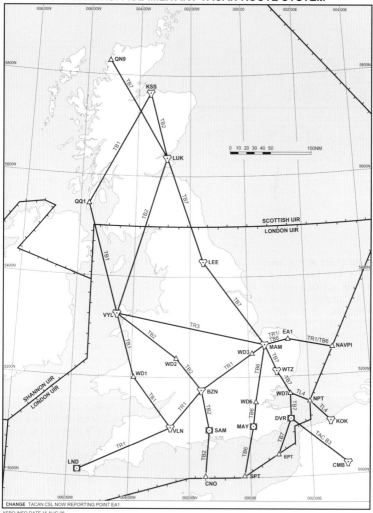

AERO INFO DATE 15 AUG 06

CHANGE TACAN CSL NOW REPORTING POINT EA1.

Upper Airspace Military Tacan
Reproduced with the permission
of the CAA, Copyright CAA

BRISTOL/CARDIFF CONTROL ZONES AND CONTROL AREAS

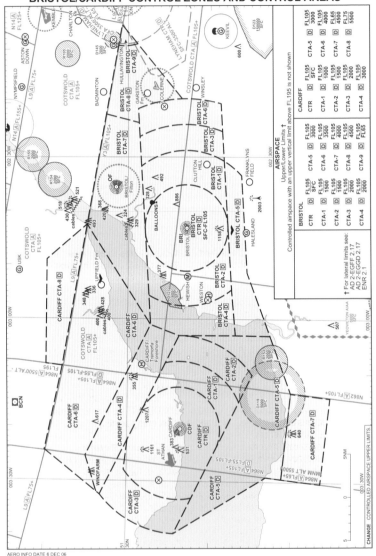

Controlled Airspace around Cardiff and Bristol

Reproduced with the permission of the CAA, copyright CAA

AERO INFO DATE 6 DEC 06

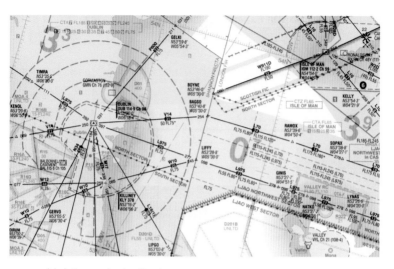

commercial air transport using the airways system and high-level routes. The charts for these two categories reflect their purpose and are completely different.

For VFR flights, pilots need to know about features on the ground, as much of their navigation will require sight of such features and landmarks. For high-level traffic, sight of the ground is largely irrelevant as the pilots will be reliant on their instruments and the waypoints set out in their flight plans.

Charts, therefore, reflect these requirements. For flights in controlled airspace, airways are defined by radio navigation beacons on the ground. These are identified by three letters, which are continuously broadcast in Morse code on the VHF radio frequency shown on the chart. Their full title is Very High Frequency Omnidirectional Radio (VOR) and their titles are taken from their location. They are usually equipped with Distance Measuring Equipment (DME) as well. For example, the Southampton VOR 'SAM' transmits the three letters in Morse on frequency 113.35 MHz. Controllers spell out the three letters 'Sierra Alpha Mike' in radio transmissions.

Different suppliers show the details in a variety of formats, using different colour schemes. Compulsory reporting points

(often coinciding with VORs) are usually shown as solid black triangles, located on route intersections or on boundaries between adjacent control areas. However, in spite of being designated as 'compulsory' not all flights actually report the fact when passing such points. 'On request' reporting points are indicated where routes intersect or where significant points exist. (EUROCONTROL uses solid triangles for all its reporting points.)

Significant Points

The NATS IAIP website (referred to earlier) contains the details of every 'significant point' in UK airspace, of which there are hundreds. They identify, by latitude and longitude, navigational points which are not supported by radio facilities on the ground. Their full title is Name Code Designators for Significant Points. They all contain five letters and are always spelt in capital letters. These points are location at intersections, changes of base levels of airways, arrival and departure routes and so on, and are used by aircraft with sophisticated navigation

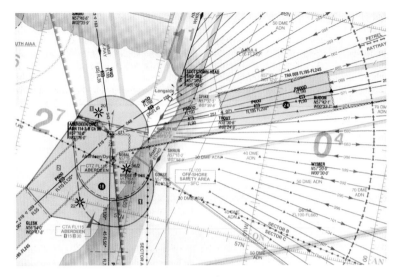

Airways in the Aberdeen/North Sea area
Reproduced by kind permission of the RAF,
OC No1 AIDU

navigation capabilities which are not dependent on radio signals for navigation.

Some of the points have a connection with place names in the vicinity – for example AMMAN (Ammanford), EXMOR (Exmoor), HALIF (Halifax), LESTA (Leicester), NEVIS (Ben Nevis), REXAM (Wrexham), WATFO (Watford), et cetera – but most are simply generated at random.

Airways and Upper Air Routes

The official terms for these are Lower Air Traffic Service Routes and Upper Air Traffic Service Routes. The Lower ATS Routes are commonly described as airways, with a defined width of at least 10 nm. The base limit of airways varies according to their purpose, usually being stepped to facilitate flights descending into terminal areas, or climbing after departure. The upper limit is FL245.

Above FL245, the Upper ATS Routes do not have a defined width, although they are nominally treated as having a width of five nm each side of the centreline. When approved by ATC, aircraft may be flown anywhere in the upper airspace and remain under positive control, whereas in lower airspace they must remain within the airway limits.

Airways and Upper ATS Routes are identified by letters and numbers, with the addition of the letter 'U' for routes in upper airspace. Usually, the same designator is used in lower and upper airspace, although the upper route may not be directly above the lower one. Every route is detailed in the NATS Aeronautical Information Publication, mentioned earlier, indicating its magnetic bearings, significant points and the distances between them.

Originally, routes were colour coded depending on their direction (green, for example, was used for east-west routes), but these disappeared many years ago and the letters used now have an international significance according to the type of route.

On 25 October 1987, to conform to international ICAO standards, the colour system was abandoned and replaced by phonetic references. Amber became Alpha, Blue became Bravo, Green became Golf, Red became Romeo, and White became Whiskey, but all these were subsequently replaced over the years.

The current designators were introduced in November 2003, to comply with the international route designator structure, when several well-known routes were retitled. For example, Golf One/Upper Golf One became Lima 9/Upper Lima 9.

Controllers may, subject to other traffic considerations, allow aircraft to track away from the upper air routes to save time and fuel; these are referred to by ATC and pilots as 'directs'. With modern navigational equipment on board flights, reference to ground-based radio stations is no longer essential so routes away from the beacons are perfectly possible.

There are relatively few airways compared to the upper routes, as the current traffic demands and the desire for better efficiency have resulted in the introduction of many new upper air routes. This has been made possible through the use of sophisticated navigation capabilities of modern aircraft which no longer rely on the traditional beacons.

An increasing number of aircraft are now routeing on direct tracks using on-board navigational equipment as opposed to ground-based aids, as part of the international strategy for increased capacity and reduced controller workload under a system referred to as Area Navigation.

National Air Traffic Services UK Integrated Aeronautical Information Package

This series of documents, often referred to as the Air Pilot, is the official publication for UK airspace. It covers all the information essential for air navigation, including route details, radio frequencies, significant

London (Swanwick) Flight Information Sectors

Reproduced with the permission of the CAA, copyright CAA

LONDON AREA CONTROL (SWANWICK) - FIS SECTORS

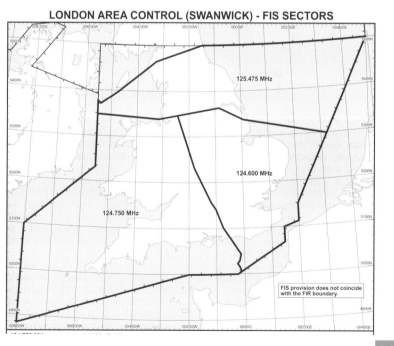

NORTHERN OCEANIC TRANSITION AREA (NOTA)

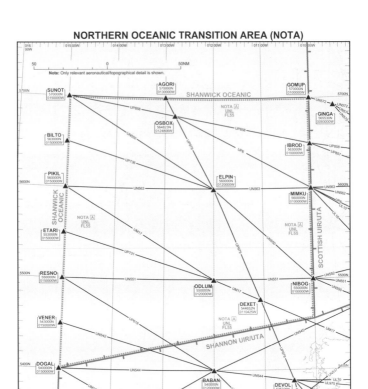

reporting points, et cetera. Notices concerning safety, navigation and technical issues are published as Circulars as and when required. Future changes and amendments due to take place in the coming weeks are published in advance on 28-day and 56-day cycles.

All this information was originally available only through an annual subscription, published in paper form and posted to each subscriber. The paper process was eventually replaced by CD, but still available only on subscription. Now, fortunately, with the development of the internet, everyone can have free access through the website.

SHANNON OCEANIC TRANSITION AREA AND RVSM TRANSITION AREA

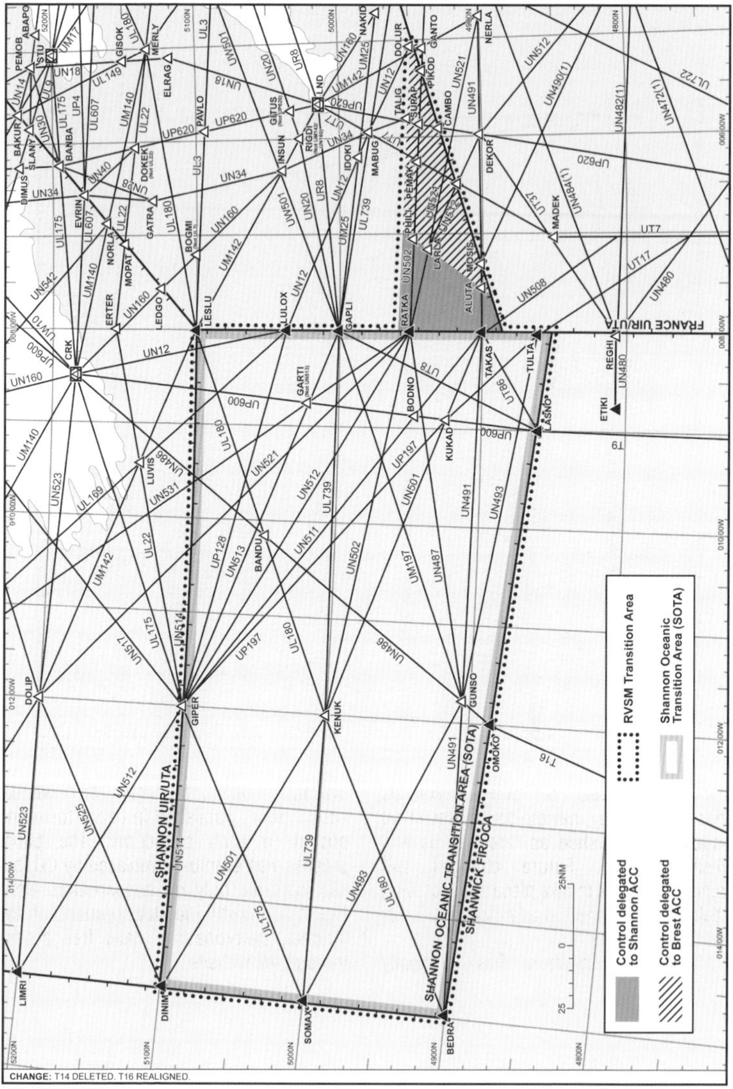

CHANGE: T14 DELETED. T16 REALIGNED.

AERO INFO DATE 28 FEB 08

Civil Aviation Authority

AMDT AIRAC 5/08

Opposite: **Northern Oceanic Transition Area**
Reproduced with the permission of the
CAA, copyright CAA

Above: **Shannon Oceanic Transition**
Reproduced with the permission of the
CAA, copyright CAA

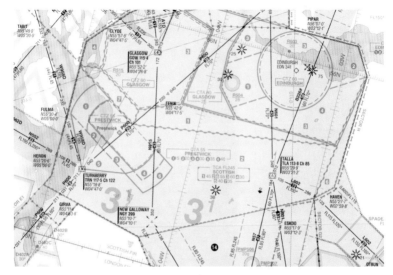

Controlled Airspace around Glasgow and Edinburgh Reproduced by kind permission of the RAF, OC No1 AIDU

Airways and Controlled Airspace in the Cardiff and Bristol area Reproduced by kind permission of the RAF, OC No1 AIDU

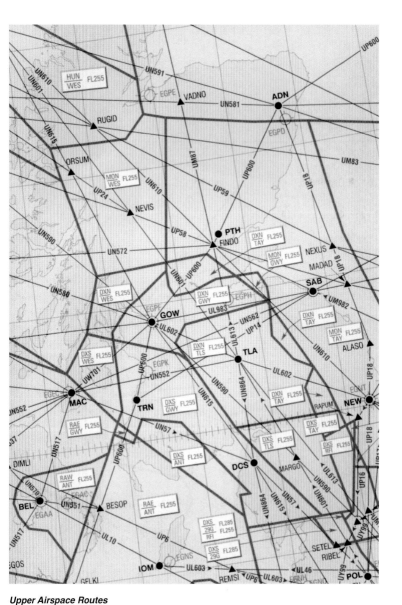

**Upper Airspace Routes
and Sectors, Scotland**
Reproduced with the permission
of EUROCONTROL

95

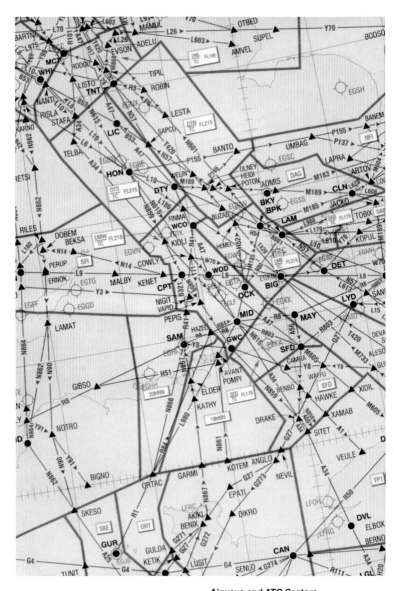

Airways and ATC Sectors,
England
Reproduced with the permission
of EUROCONTROL

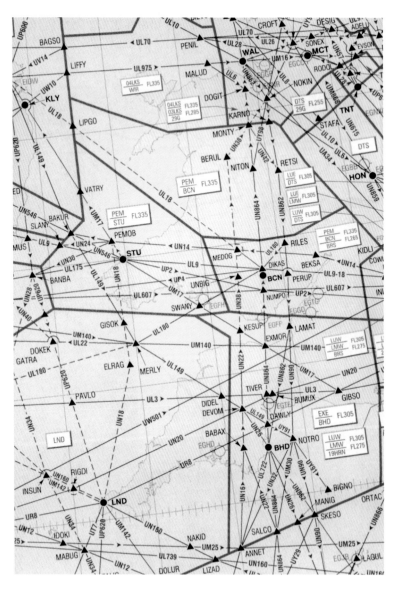

**Upper Airspace Routes and ATC Sectors,
Wales and South West England**
*Reproduced with the permission
of EUROCONTROL*

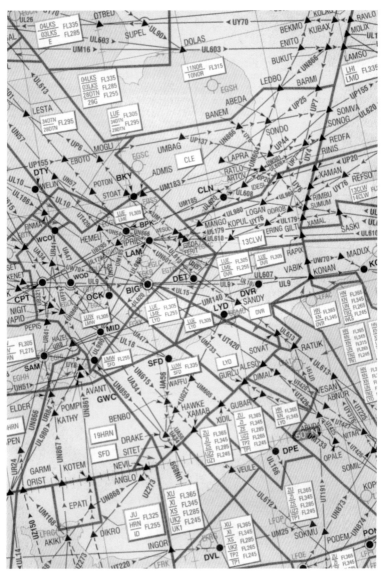

Upper Airspace Routes and ATC Sectors,
Southern England and Northern France
Reproduced with the permission
of EUROCONTROL

8. Weather and Airfield Data

Weather information for airports and forecasts of en route weather are vitally important for the safety of aviation, and a comprehensive range of meteorological services are available in the UK through a variety of processes.

Pilots have access to these by telephone, fax, datalink, the internet, dedicated VHF and UHF broadcasts and High Frequency radio. Many of the services can be accessed by the general public, free of charge.

Meteorological information for the UK is provided by the Met Office Operations Centre in Exeter, and also by local observers at airfields.

The services include:
- Pre-Flight briefings
- Terminal Aerodrome Forecasts
- Meteorological Airfield Reports
- Automatic Terminal Information Services
- Volmet.

Terminal Aerodrome Forecasts (TAF)

These reports cover forecast periods of 9, 24 and 30 hours for individual airfields, given in coded segments, using a wide variety of abbreviations to cover every conceivable situation. Details are available by telephone, fax or on the Met Office website.

There are too many codes to cover in detail here, but as an example, a wind code might be represented as follows:
'31015G25KT' which means *'Wind three one zero degrees, fifteen knots, maximum twenty five knots'*.

Meteorological Airfield Reports (METAR)

These are reports covering the actual weather conditions at individual airfields. The information is available by telephone, fax, or on the Met Office website.

Abbreviated broadcasts, which also include the runway in use, are transmitted as Automatic Terminal Information Services (ATIS) or Volmet broadcasts.

Again, a series of codes are used to cover different conditions and can be complicated and confusing at first. An example concerning cloud conditions might be:
'FEW005, SCT010CB' which represents.
'Few at five hundred feet, scattered cumulonimbus at one thousand feet'.

US Airways A330 – 323X
Shaun Grist

99

(*'Few'* means that between one and two oktas (eighths) of sky are covered; *'Scattered'* means that three to four oktas of sky are covered.)

Most UK airports have dedicated radio channels on which the ATIS message is broadcast. For airborne flights, information for any airfield may also be requested through the VHF Flight Information Service.

Automatic Terminal Information Services (ATIS)

Current conditions at airfields are available via VHF or UHF voice transmissions, or via datalink at larger airports, usually on dedicated frequencies. Details are updated at regular intervals, each message being identified by a letter which changes every time the information is updated. At larger airports arrival information and departure information are usually on separate frequencies.

Each broadcast includes the following information, where relevant:

a) *Station name* – The name by which the airport is commonly known.

b) *Time of observation* – The time of the observation in UTC.

c) *Surface wind details* – The direction of the surface wind and the speed (for example *Zero seven zero degrees one five knots*).

d) *Horizontal visibility* – Below 5,000 metres the visibility is expressed in metres (for example *Four zero zero metres*). Above 5,000 metres it is given in kilometres.

e) *Runway visual range* – In conditions of poor visibility, the runway visual range is given in metres (for example *five zero zero metres*). Where more than one runway is in use, separate RVR readings may be quoted. RVR is normally quoted for three points along the runway: touchdown, mid-point and stop-end.

f) *Weather details* – Where appropriate, a description of certain weather conditions is given in plain language (for example *rain showers, freezing rain, et cetera*).

g) *Cloud details* – Where applicable, the extent to which the sky is obscured by cloud is estimated in oktas, meaning eighths.

If the cloud cover is between one and two oktas, *'few'* is used to indicate the height of the base of the cloud layer in hundreds of feet above aerodrome level.

Where the cloud cover is between three and four oktas, *'scattered'* is used.

Where the cloud cover is between five and seven oktas, *'broken'* is used.

Where the entire sky is covered by cloud, *'overcast'* is used.

Where no cloud exists, *'sky clear'* is used.

h) *Temperature* – The temperature is given in degrees Celsius.

i) *Dew point* – The dew point is given in degrees Celsius.

j) *QNH* – QNH is given in millibars.

k) *Trend* – The trend of the weather conditions may be added if a change is expected soon. If no change is expected, an abbreviation of *'no significant change'* is given: *'No-Sig'*.

Where significant changes are expected the Trend of the forecast will be indicated by *'Becoming'* or *'Tempo'*. For example:

'BECOMING from 11.00, 25 to 35 knots, maximum 50 knots,

TEMPORARILY from 06.30 until 08.30, 3000 metres. Moderate rain showers.'

'Becoming' is used to indicate that a change is expected to take place at either a regular or irregular rate; *'Tempo'* is used to indicate a period of temporary fluctuations to the forecast conditions expected to last less than one hour.

l) *Runway state* – The runway state given at the touchdown end, mid-point and stop-end. (for example *wet, wet, wet*).

In conditions where visibility is 10 kilometres or more, there is no cumulonimbus or towering cumulus, and no cloud below 5,000ft (or the highest minimum sector altitude), and no weather likely to affect aviation, then the relevant parts of the Volmet transmission will be replaced by the expression *'Cavok'* derived from *'Cloud And Visibility OK'* and pronounced *KAV-O-KAY*.

A forecast of any significant change is included, but if none is expected, *'No-Sig'* is used.

A transcript of a typical ATIS broadcast is as follows:

'This is Heathrow Information Golf, one two five zero hours weather. Two five zero degrees, seven knots. One thousand five hundred metres. Mist. Scattered at two thousand eight hundred feet, broken at four thousand feet. Temperature five, dewpoint five. QNH one zero one five millibars. The landing runway is two seven right, departure runway two seven left. Please confirm your aircraft type and report information Golf received on first contact with Heathrow.'

Automatic Volmet

In 1981, Marconi Space and Defence Systems developed a system for transmitting weather and airfield data, which they marketed as Automatic Volmet, and since then it has been in continuous operation around the world.

The various components of the messages are digitally pre-recorded in a series of words and phrases, and these are then automatically combined into a complete report, the software selecting individual sections to suit the circumstances.

The original recordings, made by Marconi's Marketing Director at the time, were of excellent quality and it was difficult to imagine that it was not a normal human voice. Since then, other recordings have replaced the original ones, with a significant loss of quality in many cases.

In many of the original Marconi recordings, the transmission is almost identical to a normal spoken broadcast, with each word having been recorded in a typical sentence and then matched to every other word that it could be used with. For example, the same words spoken during a sentence and at the end of a sentence will sound different, with stress being applied to a greater or lesser degree. Periods of silence between words and sentences are also provided for.

The UK has three separate VHF frequencies for the London FIR, while the Scottish and Shannon FIRs each have one VHF frequency. Volmet is also available on High Frequency radio through Shannon Volmet (broadcast from Ballygirreen), which covers most European airports, while the Royal Air Force High Frequency Volmet service broadcasts similar reports on many of its operational bases around the world.

A typical Volmet broadcast, when conditions are good, is as follows:

'This is London Volmet South, this is London Volmet South. London Heathrow at one four five zero. One zero zero degrees nine knots. Cavok. Temperature nine dewpoint four. QNH one zero two five. No-Sig.'

In poor weather conditions more complicated transmission are broadcast:

'Bristol at oh five twenty zulu, wind one one zero degrees, nine knots, three hundred metres, RVR runway zero nine three hundred and fifty metres, RVR runway two seven two hundred and fifty metres, fog, broken below one hundred feet, temperature two, dewpoint two, QNH one zero two six.'

In the UK, Volmet broadcasts cover the following airfields:

London Volmet Main
Amsterdam
Brussels
Dublin
Glasgow
Gatwick
Heathrow
Stansted
Manchester
Paris (Charles de Gaulle)

London Volmet South
Birmingham
Bournemouth
Bristol
Cardiff
Jersey
Luton
Norwich
Southampton
Southend

London Volmet North
East Midlands
Humberside
Isle of Man
Leeds Bradford
Liverpool
Gatwick
Manchester
Newcastle
Durham Tees Valley

Scottish Volmet
Aberdeen
Belfast
Edinburgh
Glasgow
Inverness
Heathrow
Prestwick
Stornoway
Sumburgh

European VHF Volmet broadcasts which may be heard in parts of the UK are transmitted from Amsterdam, Brussels, Dublin and Paris.

Weather Avoidance
Other weather-related problems concern stormy weather, particularly cumulonimbus storm clouds, which can result in severe buffeting of the aircraft. Pilots will always wish to avoid such weather, and will request permission from ATC to change course accordingly.

When these conditions prevail across the country, aircraft will be changing course almost constantly as they zigzag along their route. In each of the following examples the pilot is requesting permission to change direction to avoid bad weather:

'Olympic two six six, may we turn left ten degrees to avoid weather?'

'Etihad zero one eight, may we turn left ten degrees to avoid a build-up?'

'Speedbird one five seven, may we turn left ten degrees to avoid some Charlie Bravos?

Speedbird one five seven, left turn approved, advise me when resuming own navigation.'

Note that the correct word in this last example is *'approved'* and not *'cleared'*; this is because the pilot made the request.

Dragonair B747 – 412 BCF
Shaun Grist

9. The Next Twenty Years

In 2008, EUROCONTROL produced *Challenges of Growth*, its third forecast for twenty years ahead, predicting traffic levels across the continent and attempting to tackle important constraints affecting future safety levels, pollution and capacity. Although its assessment was more optimistic than the earlier forecasts produced in 2001 and 2004, it still anticipated a shortfall in capacity with as many as two million flights in 2030 being unable to fly from the airports and at the times preferred by the airlines.

This is expected to be the case even taking into account a 40 per cent increase in capacity over the same period. These 'unaccommodated' flights would have to operate from alternative airports or at less busy times – or both – even though this would not be the most convenient for passengers.

Many initiatives are underway to meet these challenges, with several new developments in technology, co-operation between air navigation service providers and important initiatives towards the concept of the 'Single Sky for Europe'.

The Single European Sky Air Traffic Management Research programme (SESAR) has now moved into the development stage which will be completed in the next three years, after which the deployment phase will see the implementation of new systems and procedures that are expected to increase capacity in Europe by a factor of three.

The Single European Sky initiative aims to do away with the restraints imposed by having more than 40 separate organisations across Europe responsible for air traffic management, handling around 10 million flights from 75 control centres, many of them using different systems and products. Compare this with the United States, where around 30 control centres deal with over 20 million flights.

However, these changes will need a huge commitment on all sides. Airlines are reluctant to invest in costly new systems unless they can see tangible benefits in fuel burn, safety and reduced pollution, and with 38 separate States across the continent, reaching agreements on the way forward is not always easy.

IFACTS clearance window depicting a potential conflict between Ryanair 4132 and Aer Lingus 683. The options for the controller are shown on the right-hand panel, with proposed heading, speed and level changes. Any of these may be selected by the controller as a 'what if' scenario to resolve the conflict NATS

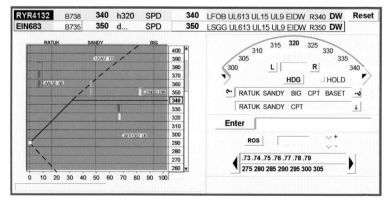

Nevertheless, major advances are being made and new working methods are being introduced as technology moves ahead, providing the means for the ATC system to cope with increasing traffic levels at the same, or even better, levels of safety.

Some of these developments are examined in the next few pages.

IFACTS

In 2009, an important tool for providing controllers with advance warning of potential conflicts was introduced at the London Area Control Centre, Swanwick. The system, known as IFACTS (Interim Future Air Traffic Control Tools Support), developed by NATS in collaboration with Praxis and Lockheed Martin, is a series of computerised predictive tools that have been described as the most significant advance in ATC since radar was introduced.

Controllers are provided with flight information that enables them to deal with larger numbers of aircraft than previously, warning them about flights which are not keeping to their flight plans, and issuing Medium Term Conflict Alerts of potential problems up to 20 minutes in advance.

The system uses electronic flight progress strips instead of traditional paper strips, checking radar-derived information on flights which may be in a future conflict, giving controllers time to assess the best course of action in a 'what-if' scenario.

The tools are named 'Interim' as they are a forerunner of the next generation Flight Data Processing System which will increase UK capacity to enable an extra three quarters of a million flights to be accommodated by 2013. The three elements are:

- Trajectory prediction
- Medium Term Conflict Detection
- Flight Path Monitoring.

Aircraft are presented on radar, in plan and section views, indicating the point at which the conflict could occur, with the predicted separation at their closest point. The controller can input a solution well in advance – perhaps a level or heading change – and the software checks to determine if this could affect other traffic. The results are displayed on screen as a text box indicating the separation which can be achieved as a consequence of the controller's action.

The Flight Path Monitoring element monitors the actions taken by the crews in complying with any ATC instructions and alerts the controllers to any deviation.

Traffic Merging of Arrivals

Improvements in the sequencing and merging of aircraft making an approach to an airport are possible through a concept known as 'Point Merge' where individual flights arrange their own distances from other traffic through the use of Precision Area Navigation (P-RNAV) equipment. It also allows more efficient and quieter continuous descent approaches, even in busy airspace.

Under the system, each flight is cleared to a specific navigation point by ATC, with an instruction to 'merge' with another aircraft, identified by the controller by its squawk code. The pilot inputs the code into the Flight Management System, together with the required separation in seconds. The FMS automatically communicates with the transponder of the other aircraft and establishes the planned separation to be achieved, even though both aircraft may still be many miles apart.

The FMS then 'merges' the two aircraft, separated by the required time, and brings them onto the final approach. Successive flights carry out the same procedure, smoothing the flow of traffic into one orderly stream.

Advanced Flight Data Processing System

A new approach towards reducing the problems caused by Europe's fragmented ATC system, by improving interoperability between states, was introduced at the Maastricht Upper Area Control Centre at the end of December 2008. This is the first implementation in Europe, having been developed in accordance with internationally agreed standards.

London Area Control Centre, Swanwick
NATS

The new Flight Data Processing System operates on a completely new philosophy, using the aircraft trajectory information to continuously update the path of the flight and calculate its most efficient route while at the same time automatically passing the amended details to other sectors and control centres along the route. This is a complete departure from the traditional method where aircraft follow a fairly rigid route through the airspace according to their flight plans.

With the new system, the trajectory initially requested by the aircraft is automatically updated through radar returns and inputs from the controllers, adjusting to the best flight profile based on real-time feedback. It also improves safety and efficiency, together with reducing pollution.

The FDPS also includes a Medium Term Conflict Prediction tool, warning controllers of possible conflicts up to 20 minutes ahead, giving them time to decide on the best solution and amend the flight profile accordingly.

Other features include automatic monitoring of clearances, informing the controller if the aircraft changes heading or level, improved datalink communications enabling messages to be passed to the pilot with a single mouse click, easy rearrangement of sectors to match traffic loading or weather conditions, and monitoring of controllers' workload across the sectors.

Automatic Dependent Surveillance – Broadcast (ADS-B)

ADS-B is an advanced surveillance system which will be an essential element of the EUROCONTROL SESAR and the Federal Aviation Authority NextGen programmes, eventually enabling flights to maintain their own separation and to optimise flight trajectories.

The system works by broadcasting an aircraft's identity, position and velocity to other aircraft and to the ground, using satellite technology to produce a highly accurate and reliable picture to Air Traffic Control and to adjacent flights. This information is used to compute the safest and most efficient track of each aircraft, independently of any ground-based input, with ATC providing a monitoring and managing role of the overall picture.

ADS-B transmits information twice every second, and when the details are presented on the controller's radar screen, the display informs the controller how the information was derived, either by radar or by ADS-B. Trials have shown that ADS-B provides a higher degree of accuracy than traditional radar.

Automatic Dependent Surveillance has been in use on North Sea helicopter routes since 1990, transmitting position data to control units via the Inmarsat satellite. One major benefit is the ability to operate perfectly well down to sea level, well below the range of normal radar.

Several airlines have already received approval to use ADS-B as the sole method of surveillance in regions not covered by radar, and the system will also be introduced in European airspace from 2009 onwards as the first step towards the concept of 'Free Flight', where flight paths are determined by the on-board equipment.

'Free Flight involves airspace without fixed route structures in which suitably equipped aircraft will be able to fly user preferred four dimensional routes and may take responsibility for their own separation. The eventual situation will be that all aircraft will be able to fly under Free Flight mode. Access to this airspace by less capable aircraft will be subject to acceptance by the Air Traffic Management Services whereby access by capable aircraft is implicit. Free Flight mode is defined as operations comprising both free routeing and autonomous separation.'
(EUROCONTROL definition)

Airborne Collision Avoidance Systems

The Airborne Collision Avoidance System (ACAS) is an independent safety net already mandatory in most parts of the world. It provides an independent warning of potential collisions between aircraft where the ATC system has failed to detect a problem.

The only system approved for worldwide use is the Traffic Alert and Collision Avoidance System (TCAS) and it has demonstrated its effectiveness by a considerable reduction in the number of air misses in spite of increasing traffic levels. However, flight crews have to understand the system and its operating principles if it is to function correctly, and this involves careful training and monitoring by the national authorities.

The aviation world was shocked when a mid-air collision occurred in European airspace in July 2002, even though traffic levels were low at the time. Although a number of factors were involved, one of them highlighted the fact that the training in the use of TCAS is critical if the system is to be effective. The investigation soon discovered that the TCAS on both aircraft operated correctly and if the flight crew on one of the aircraft had responded correctly, the disaster would almost certainly have been avoided.

TCAS works by interrogating the transponders of other aircraft in the area, checking to determine if any of them are a threat, and issuing warnings to the pilots, instructing them to take evasive action if a collision is a possibility.

The warnings, known as Resolution Advisories (RAs), operate in the vertical plane only, advising pilots to climb or descend. TCAS information updates every second, so the information it produces is more up to date than a radar screen on the ground; therefore pilots should always follow an RA command even if it conflicts with an ATC instruction. This is what happened in the case described earlier, where the pilot of one aircraft decided to ignore an RA instruction to climb the aircraft and instead followed the controller's message to descend, with catastrophic results.

Part of the reason for this fatal course of action was the initial training given by the aviation authority responsible for the flight, which advised its pilots that they should do what the controller says at all times, ignoring the better advice produced by TCAS.

Another aspect highlighted in this case was the fact that controllers are unable to detect RAs through radar, and depend on pilots informing them verbally. In extremely tense situations this may be forgotten and controllers may issue contradictory instructions in an attempt to resolve the situation.

Experiments into downloading RA events to the controller's radar have been taking place for several years, but so far no decision on its implementation has been made.

Advanced Surveillance Systems

There are two levels of surveillance available through Mode S transponders: Elementary and Enhanced.

Mode S (meaning Selective) is an advanced type of transponder capable of being interrogated from the ground for a variety of information. Responses are then transmitted by datalink, independently of the pilots.

Enhanced surveillance was introduced in terminal airspace and on major routes in the UK in March 2005. This permits elementary interrogation by controllers of a selection of Downlink Aircraft Parameters, consisting of the squawk, the aircraft altitude to the nearest 25ft, the callsign, and the status of the flight. Each aircraft is allocated a 24-bit unique identifier, which means that the interrogation will be received only by that specific aircraft. The enhanced mode enables extra data to be obtained, including ground speed, track angle, turn rate, roll angle, climb rate, magnetic heading, indicated air speed or Mach number and selected flight level.

Elementary surveillance was introduced in the rest of UK airspace in 2008.

Summary

New initiatives continue to be developed worldwide, aiming to address capacity bottlenecks, safety and the growing pressure to deal with environmental issues. Most rely on the use of better technology, both in the air and on the ground, which will move the management of air traffic towards a joint responsibility between ATC and pilots.

10. Appendix: Useful Contacts

Air Traffic Control Centres

London Area Control Centre
Sopwith Way
Swanwick
Southampton
Hampshire SO31 7AY
Tel: 01489 584875

Scottish and Oceanic Air Traffic Control Centre
Atlantic House
Sherwood Road
Prestwick
Ayrshire KA9 2NR
Tel: 01292 479800

Manchester Area Control Centre
Manchester Airport
Wythenshawe,
Manchester M90 2PL
Tel: 0161 499 5300

Main Organisations

National Air Traffic Services Ltd
Corporate and Technical Centre
4000 Parkway
Whiteley
Fareham
Hants PO15 7FL
www.nats.co.uk

Civil Aviation Authority
CAA House
45-59 Kingsway
London WC2B 6TE
Tel: 020 7379 7311
www.caa.co.uk

UK Aeronautical Information Service
Heathrow House
Bath Road
Hounslow
Middlesex TW5 9AT
Tel: 020 8745 3456
www.nats-uk.ead-it.com

Irish Aviation Authority
Aviation House
Hawkins Street
Dublin 2
Ireland
Tel: 353 1 6031100
www.iaa.ie

International Civil Aviation Organization,
1000 Sherbrooke Street West
Suite 400
Montreal
Quebec
Canada H3A 2R2
Tel: (514) 285 8222
www.icao.int

EUROCONTROL
European Organisation for the Safety of Air Navigation
Rue de la Fusee 96
B-1130 Brussels
Tel: 32.2.729 90 11
www.eurocontrol.int

College of Air Traffic Control
National Air Traffic Services
Bournemouth (Hurn) Airport
Christchurch
Dorset BH23 6DF
Tel: 01202 472334

Charts and Publications Suppliers

Airplan Flight Equipment
1A Ringway Trading Estate
Shadowmoss Road
Manchester M22 5LH
Tel: 0161 499 0023
Fax: 0161 499 0298
www.afeonline.com

European Aeronautical Group UK Ltd
Hersham House
Lyon Road
Walton-on-Thames
Surrey KT12 3PU
Tel: 01932 704200
Fax: 01932 267572
www.euronautical.com

Royal Air Force
Flight Information Publications
No 1 AIDU
RAF Northolt
West End Road
Ruislip
Middlesex HA4 6NG
Tel: 020 8845 2300
Fax: 020 8841 1078
www.aidu.mod.uk

Eurocontrol Cartography Service
www.eurocontrol.int/carto/public/subsite_
homepage/homepage.html

Transair Pilot Shop
Shoreham Airport
Shoreham-by-Sea,
West Sussex BN43 5PA
Tel: 01273 466000
www.transair.co.uk

Finnair Airbus A319
Author